AF704006

Dean Kingham has practised prison law since 2006. He initially qualified as a Barrister but chose to cross-qualify as a solicitor and was admitted to the roll in 2011. He has a number of roles within the Criminal Justice System as part of his prisoners right practice, including being an Executive Committee Member for the Association of Prison lawyers for which he acts as joint Parole Board lead, which allows him to sit on the Parole Board User Group, he is a committee member for Progressing Prisoners Maintaining Innocence and is a council member for the Human Rights Charity Justice. In 2020, he was named public law legal aid lawyer of the year, which recognised the fact he is often at the forefront of the challenging and advancing prisoner rights.

John Turner is a former Chair of the Association of Prison lawyers. Along with Dean, he is currently joint Parole Board lead for the Association of Prison lawyers and sits on the Parole Board User Group. He has practiced in prison law since 2004 and frequently appears before the Parole Board. John has also written and offered training on issues relating to prison law. Like Dean, John has acted in many key and high-profile prison law cases and has been involved in public law challenges concerning prisoners' rights in both the domestic courts as well as in the European Court of Human Rights.

A Practical Guide to Parole Board Proceedings

A Practical Guide to Parole Board Proceedings

Dean Kingham, Solicitor

John Turner, Solicitor

Law Brief Publishing

Published 2024 by Law Brief Publishing, an imprint of Law Brief Publishing Ltd
30 The Parks
Minehead
Somerset
TA24 8BT

www.lawbriefpublishing.com

Paperback: 978-1-916698-50-5

PREFACE

John and I have both practised prison law for in excess of 15 years and in light of the significant changes to the parole process we thought we would write a simple guide to Parole Board proceedings. Realising we are now both nearer to the end of our careers rather than the start we thought it was appropriate to provide a handy easy to read reference guide for anyone with an interest in parole.

When we both started out conducting parole work the Board's work was little known. Over more recent years transparency has become a big feature and now on occasion people can observe public parole hearings, along with programmes being made about the Board's work so it feels a lot more open. However, the Parole Board rules set by the Secretary of State for Justice along with processes are not so well known and we both felt this book was needed more than ever. In recent years, we have seen reconsideration, setting aside, allegation consideration to name but a few be added to the Parole Board work and thus the work of the Board is now more complex than ever.

On average, we both appear in oral hearings before the Board approximately 120 times per year and have represented the most serious, complex and notorious prisoners and represent hundreds of prisoners per year. We have both been at the forefront of developments of the parole system and taken a number of different Judicial Review challenges for prisoners. John, has represented prisoners in the European Court of Human Rights.

Thus, we both feel that there is nothing we haven't encountered, seen or been able to deal with it. We wanted to impart our experience and provide a handy guide.

We have both sat on the Executive Committee for the Association of Prison lawyers for a number of years, with John previously having been the Chair. We both sit on the Parole Board User Group as a result and join working parties to assist ensure the system remains prisoner focused and rights are protected.

We both record a regular podcast covering relevant prison law issues under the prison lawyers name so if this book has made you want to engage more with parole, do listen to our episodes.

The authors believe that the law stated is correct and up-to-date as of 16th September 2024.

Dean Kingham
September 2024

CONTENTS

Chapter One	Introduction	1
Chapter Two	Parole Board Rules and Published Guidance	7
Chapter Three	Recall	13
Chapter Four	The Parole Board Review Process	21
Chapter Five	Hearings	33
Chapter Six	Post-Hearing	59
Concluding Remarks		71
Appendix	The Parole Board Rules	73

CHAPTER ONE

INTRODUCTION

The Parole Board was created in 1996 and is an executive non departmental public body (NDPB). As an NDPB the Board is sponsored by the Ministry of Justice.

It is not therefore a Government Department but operates at arm's length from ministers. The Board's rules are ultimately created by the Ministry of Justice. A clear set of Parole Board Rules governing the entirety of the Board's work is contained within the Parole Boards 2019, amended in July 2022.

The Parole Board is, in law, considered a Court, but it has nowhere near the same powers as a Court. As a result of the above, concerns have been raised as to whether it is sufficiently independent of the executive.

Whilst being considered a court it has no enforcement powers and, as such, if directions are not complied with panels are often frustrated they have little/no power to take steps to ensure compliance. Many believe the Parole Board should move within the HM Court and Tribunal Service and be given full powers.

In 2018, a prisoner Mr. Wakenshaw challenged the manner in which the Chair of the Parole Board was removed by the then Justice Secretary following a case involving a high-profile prisoner, which raised concern. Mr. Wakenshaw was concerned as to the fairness of the system and whether he could have a procedurally fair hearing before the Parole Board. The High Court decided that it is arguable that the Parole Board lacked "objective independence" from the Government because of the arrangements that were in place by which members of the Board could be removed from their position by the Secretary of State. Changes have since been made following the judgement in R (Wakenshaw) v Secretary of State for Justice (SSJ) [2018] EWHC 2089 (Admin).

The independence of the Board has been further tested as a result of differing approaches by various Secretary of State for Justice. Mr. Raab who held office when the last Root and Branch review of the Parole Board's work was published in March 2022 made clear in the foreword to the report:

> "*In recent years, a number of decisions to release offenders who have committed heinous crimes have led to a loss of public confidence in the parole system. People have questioned how safe it really is to release certain offenders and why those recalled to prison were allowed to leave in the first place. I share these concerns, which is why I am determined to re-focus the system to put public protection at the forefront of all parole decisions. The statutory test has therefore changed over time to become a 'balancing exercise' between the rights of the prisoner to be considered for release and the responsibility of the state to protect the public*".

The Parole Board has a single statutory test, which is: Is it necessary for the protection of the public that the individual remains confined? It is a pure public protection test. There is no balancing exercise it is solely public protection.

The Parole Board can only act on the terms of each individual referral made by the Secretary of State for Justice delated to the Public Protection Casework section (PPCS) and the Board's options will vary on the type of case it is considering.

It will either be able to consider whether to direct release or make a recommendation for open conditions or just release.

When assessing open conditions, the Parole Board plays an advisory function. The SSJ can therefore lawfully reject a recommendation of the

Board if it does so on rational grounds. There has been extensive case law in this area following a number of challenges by prisoners.

The success of the challenges has turned on the individual factual circumstances.

In Green, R (On the Application Of) v Secretary of State for Justice (No 2) [2023] EWHC 1211 (Admin) (22 May 2023), the High Court indicated the following would need to apply in order for the SSJ to disagree with a recommendation from the Board:

i. the Secretary of State must accord weight to the Parole Board's recommendations, although the weight to be given depends on the matters in issue, the type of hearing before the panel, its findings and the nature of the assessment of risk it had to make;

ii. on matters in respect of which the Parole Board enjoys a particular advantage over the Secretary of State (such as fact finding), he must give clear, cogent, and convincing reasons for departing from these;

iii. with other matters such as the assessment of risk, where the Secretary of State is exercising an evaluative judgment, he must accord appropriate respect to the view of the Parole Board and he must still give reasons for departing from it, but he can only be challenged on conventional public law grounds such as irrationality, unfairness, failure to apply policy, and not taking material considerations into account.

Over the last few years, as a result of political tinkering, the Ministry of Justice has changed the test for open conditions a number of times. Currently, in in order to consider open conditions the Board must make a recommendation to the SSJ considering the following tests:

i. the extent to which the indeterminate sentence prisoner (ISP) has made sufficient progress during the sentence in addressing and reducing risk to a level consistent with protecting the public from harm, in circumstances where the ISP in open conditions may be in the community, unsupervised, under licensed temporary release; and

ii. the prisoner is assessed as low risk of abscond;

In considering whether or not to accept the recommendation the SSJ himself considers whether a 'wholly persuasive' case exists. 'Wholly persuasive' has not been defined and it has been difficult to establish a true definition.

For many lifers open conditions is a real and meaningful resettlement opportunity which enables them to slowly and safely reintegrate into the community. Over the last few years the number of life sentence prisoners transferred to open conditions has dropped significantly. It is troubling that there is no real marker as to how risky lifers in open conditions actually are as the fact the Ministry of Justice does not keep re-offending data for those in the open estate.

A foreign national indeterminate sentence prisoner (FNP) (ISP) who is being served with a deportation order and who has exhausted all their UK appeal rights is not eligible to be considered for open conditions. An indeterminate sentence prisoner who is liable for deportation but who has not exhausted their appeal rights may still be considered for transfer to open conditions. For such prisoners the Parole Board must be satisfied that they present a very low risk of abscond. this is a higher test then the low risk of abscond for ordinary ISP prisoners.

Every case referred to the Parole Board is required to go through the Member Case Assessment (MCA) process. MCA is often described as 'triage' because each case, at the earliest opportunity (the point of referral), is considered by a Parole Board member who determines whether the prisoner can be released, whether an oral hearing is required or whether the case can be concluded on the papers. Naturally, we will go into further detail later within this book.

At MCA stage the case is considered by a single member. If the case is considered high-profile or if it is related to terrorism then the case is allocated to a specialist cohort of members.

The entire work of the Parole Board is governed by the Parole Board Rules and the Board's own guidance.

CHAPTER TWO

PAROLE BOARD RULES AND PUBLISHED GUIDANCE

There are now a total of 31 rules the Parole Board are governed by. The Board publishes guidance to members as to how it interprets these rules. Its guidance is wide ranging. Reference will be made to the most relevant guidance within this book.

We do not intend to take you through each and every Parole Board Rule because that would be incredibly dull, particularly given that they are readily accessible online. However, we will touch upon the most important Parole Board Rules throughout the course of the book.

Summary of the Parole Board rules

- Rules 1-4 cover application, interpretation and appointments.

- Rule 5 covers the appointment of panels. In every case that is referred to the Board the Chair of the Parole Board must appoint one or more members of the Board to comprise a panel to consider the release of a prisoner on the papers, this is know as the Member Case Assessment (MCA) stage.

- Rule 6 deals with case management and covers the powers that members have to make, vary and revoke directions to them to manage cases.

- Rule 7 of the Parole Board rules covers case conferences and directions hearings.

- Rule 9 is particularly crucial to practitioners because it provides the mechanism for duty members or panel chairs to alter time limits within the rules. This is obviously useful for issues such as observer requests, witness requests etc.

- Rule 10 focuses on legal representation and allows prisoners to appoint someone to act on their behalf. It also gives the Panel Chair and Duty Members the power to appoint a representative for the prisoner with their agreement or, where the prisoner does not have capacity, allows for a representative to be appointed if it is in the prisoner's best interests to be represented.

- Rules 11 and 12 relate to method of service and date of service. The most utilised method of service is to provide material/documents to an email address within the Parole Board. Most commonly this is to the case manager dealing with the case. Rule 12 makes it clear that unless a duty member or panel chair states otherwise, any document served under Rule 11 is deemed served the next working day after the documents were sent. The rules provide clear guidance on date of service for postal documents, but we have not set them out here as the bulk of the Parole Board's work is now dealt with electronically.

- Rules 13 and 14 covers Witnesses and Observers. Rule 13 makes clear that a request to call a witness at an oral hearing must be made within a written application no later than 12 weeks before the date of the oral hearing. The time limit is the same for observers under rule 14.

- Rule 16 deals with the referral and provides that the case is deemed to have been referred to the Board at the point that the referral and all necessary information is received from the Secretary of State.

- Rule 17 covers non-disclosure and sets out the procedures for withholding information from the prisoner and/or their legal representative.

- Rule 18 covers the procedures for the parties making representations to the Board and for serving any additional evidence.

- Rule 19 gives panels the power to make a decision on the papers or to direct an oral hearing.

- Rule 20 covers the procedure for prisoners who have been found unsuitable for release on the papers to then apply for an oral hearing.

- Rule 21 provides that, if a direction has been made for a case to be considered at an oral hearing, a panel chair or duty member can conclude that review on the papers if further information is provided that would make an oral hearing unnecessary.

- Rules 22 to 24 set out the procedures for cases that are to be considered at an oral hearing.

- Rule 25–27 covers release decisions following an oral hearing, this being a decision of the majority of the panel. Rule 27 covers decision summaries.

- Rules 28–30 covers the reconsideration mechanism, setting aside and the slip rule.

- Rule 31 covers applications to terminate IPP licences.

Parole Board decision making framework

The Parole Board has published a decision-making guide to ensure consistency amongst members but, in doing so, makes it clear that it insists on individual professional judgement in reaching decisions.

The guidance makes clear that the Board is not concerned with involving itself in the punitive element of a sentence. The Board only concerns itself with the risk of serious harm, risk of reoffending and any other relevant factors to allow it to make an informed assessment of risk. As such it considers risk factors applicable to the individual prisoner along with any protective factors.

A risk factor is described as "*aspects of the prisoner's life that have inclined them towards harmful behaviour*".

A protective factor is described as "*an aspect of the prisoner's life that have inclined them away from harmful behaviour*".

The guidance does not attempt to set out an exhaustive list of issues/matters that a Parole Board panel will consider, but does pose the following questions that panels are encouraged to consider:

- What further offence(s) might the prisoner commit?
- Will they cause serious harm?
- Who might the victim(s) be?
- What features might contribute to serious harm (the risk factors)?
- What might protect against serious harm (the protective factors)?
- How and when could the above factors combine, either to increase or decrease risk (scenario planning)?

- How probable is a high-risk scenario (likelihood)?
- How soon could a further serious offence take place (imminence)?
- What measures can be put in place to reduce the likelihood and/or degree of harm occurring (risk management plan)?

It is important to acknowledge that the Board cannot consider cases of its own back. In order to consider a case, the Secretary of State must refer the matter to the Parole Board. The SSJ only refers certain types of cases to the Parole Board.

The Parole Board is empowered to make decisions about the following:

- Deciding whether to release indeterminate sentence prisoners on or after the end of their tariff;
- Deciding whether to release some categories of determinate-sentence prisoners;
- Deciding whether some recalled prisoners should be re-released;
- Advising the Secretary of State as to whether an indeterminate-sentence prisoner should progress to an open prison; and
- Advising on any other matter relating to release or recall that the Secretary of State refers to the Board.

This means that the Parole Board's work includes prisoners who have not been released and are seeking parole and people who have been released, but have been recalled to custody for breaching the licence conditions imposed upon them at the point of release.

CHAPTER THREE

RECALL

Recall prisoners are those that have been released on licence who have then been recalled to prison by the Probation Service as authorised by the Secretary of State for Justice.

They may well be determinate sentence recalls, extended sentence recalls or life sentence recalls.

An individual can be recalled for an alleged breach of their licence conditions.

In recall cases the Parole Board is duty bound to consider the appropriateness of the recall in accordance with the rest set out in R(Calder) v Secretary of State for Justice [2015] EWCA Civ 1050 7 2. The Board has to assess the lawfulness of the recall. Calder established a two-part test:

i) Was the Secretary of State entitled to conclude on the evidence available that the applicant was in breach of his licence conditions?

ii) Were the reasons given by the Secretary of State adequate?

Whether the SSJ was entitled to conclude on the available evidence that the individual had breached their licence conditions is obviously fact specific. It is important to carefully consider the evidence and form a view on whether this is the case.

In assessing the material the Parole Board will consider factors such as:

- Whether licence conditions were breached;

- Whether the breach was intentional;
- The seriousness of the breach;
- The circumstances of the breach, including any mitigating factors that reduce the fault of the prisoner;
- The strength of the evidence of the breach and any other evidence supporting the decision to recall;
- The relevance of the recall incident to risk; and
- Other information relating to the recall that is available to the Parole Board.

It is important to emphasise that this list is by no means exhaustive

Particular challenges arise when an individual has been suspected of having committed an offence and has been questioned by police. It is extremely common to see people recalled following arrest but before charge. We commonly deal with individuals who are released pending further enquiries or where no further action has been taken. In such cases it is important to focus on what information the Probation Service and SSJ had at the time that the decision to recall was taken and authorised.

A standard licence condition that is used as a catch all is "*They shall be of good behaviour and not behave in a way which undermines the purpose of the licence period*". "Good behaviour" is not defined and whether someone has not been of good behaviour is fact specific.

In assessing the first part of the Calder test you may find the following cases helpful:

Broadbent v The Parole Board of England and Wales [2005] EWHC 1207 (Admin) (27 May 2005) the High Court makes clear:

> *"Nonetheless I am clear that the fact of a charge and a pending prosecution alone cannot without more justify a conclusion that there is a risk of reoffending....... Moreover, if the fact of a charge and a prosecution for the offence was sufficient, it is difficult to see how the Board could give to the prisoner the fair hearing to which he is entitled, as envisaged by the House of Lords in R (Smith and West) v The Parole Board [2005] UKHL 1".*

R (on the application of McHale) v Secretary of State for Justice [2010] EWHC 3657, at 16 Mr Justice Langstaff notes:

> *"It would seem to me to be offensive that a prisoner should be assumed to have committed an offence merely because he had been charged with it; the charge itself is something of which he must be presumed innocent unless and until proved guilty".*

In Gulliver v The Parole Board [2007] EWCA Civ 1386 the Court of Appeal made clear:

> *"The recall of a prisoner is not a punishment, and thus not the determination of a criminal charge for the purposes of article 6 of the European Convention on Human Rights ("the Convention"); see R (Smith (No 2) and West) v The Parole Board [2005] 1 WLR 350 paragraphs 46, 56, 76, 90 and 91 and The purpose of recall is to protect the public against risk. R v Sharkey [2000] 1WLR 160 at 162h-163b, Smith and West paragraph 26".*

In R (Jorgenson) v Secretary of State for Justice [2011] EWHC 977, Silber J concluded at paragraph 16 that it was not every breach of a licence which would justify a decision to recall an offender:

> *"In my view, in every case where the Secretary of State could reasonably conclude there has been a breach, he or she must then proceed to consider as an important free-standing separate issue,*

> *which is what steps should be taken to deal with this breach. In other words, the mere fact that a prisoner released on licence is in breach of his/her licence or is reasonably believed to be in breach does not mean that recall must automatically be ordered. Of course, in many cases there will be no difficulty in concluding that the Secretary of State was entitled to order recall such as where the licensee has committed identical offences to those for which he was originally sentenced."*

Upon the first review following recall the Parole Board will consider whether, with reference to the Calder test, the recall was appropriate?

Following, that first review the Parole Board is not under a duty at subsequent reviews to look again at the appropriateness of the recall, although can do so if some further information/evidence comes to light that would likely have an impact on the original decision.

In the majority of cases, the Parole Board will already be considering the circumstances around recall because it goes directly to consideration of risk. If the recall is not disputed then the Board need not spend too long looking at the appropriateness of the recall.

It may not be possible to make such a determination on the papers as there may well be a need to hear oral evidence from witnesses or to request further information/reports. The Parole Board will make its assessment of risk on the basis of all the evidence. For practitioners, it is vitally important to consider what evidence would be of assistance to the Parole Board. If the individual is suspected of having committed an offence, do you require information pertaining to that allegation? Will it assist/advance your client's case?

Practitioners representing recalled clients will want to carefully consider how the recall goes to risk. Not every recall will go directly to the risk of serious harm and often will be related to the individual's compliance with licence conditions.

When submitting representations at the MCA stage do not be afraid to seek directions for information/reports that you consider are relevant to the issues to be explored.

If the Parole Board make a finding that the recall was inappropriate, and/or there was no breach of licence it does not necessarily follow that the Parole Board must release the prisoner. This is because the Parole Board will still need to carefully assess the current level of risk posed and any perceived future risk in considering the statutory release test. A good example of this is where the reasons for recall upon exploration were flawed, but other information has come to light following the recall or where there are custodial conduct issues, which means the statutory release test is not met.

Any decision taken by the Parole Board on the appropriateness of recall must be sufficiently set out in writing. The rationale for a decision must be sufficiently reasoned for the reader of the decision to properly understand. In reviewing decisions it is often helpful for practitioners to remined themselves of the following passage from the the House of Lords Judgment in <u>South Bucks District Council v Porter</u> <u>[2003] EWCA Civ 687:</u>

> *"The reasons for a decision must be intelligible and they must be adequate. They must enable the reader to understand why the matter was decided as it was and what conclusions were reached on the "principal important controversial issues", disclosing how any issue of law or fact was resolved. Reasons can be briefly stated, the degree of particularity required depending entirely on the nature of the issues falling for decision. The reasoning must not give rise to a substantial doubt as to whether the decision-maker erred in law, for example by misunderstanding some relevant policy or some other important matter or by failing to reach a rational decision on relevant grounds".*

Risk Period

The period over which panels are considering risk is indefinite for both indeterminate and determinate sentence cases. In other words, in determinate sentence cases, it includes risk posed by the prisoner to the public during the sentence and after the sentence has expired. This applies irrespective of whether the case to be considered is at initial release or re-release following recall.

In Johnson EWHC 1282 (Admin), the Court determined that the statutory test for release has no temporal element. The test is whether release would cause a more than minimal risk of serious harm to the public at any time. Therefore, consideration of risk for determinate sentence prisoners goes beyond conditional release dates (CRD) and sentence expiry dates (SED). While the case before the court concerned an extended determinate sentence (EDS) prisoner, the principles set out within the judgment apply to all determinate sentence cases. This is because the statutory test is the same in all cases.

In assessing the necessity of continuing detention in determinate sentence cases (on both initial release and after recall), the focus must be on the consequences of early release:

- If release before the date of automatic release would clearly significantly increase the risk of serious harm to the public, (relative to continuing detention), irrespective of when the actual harm might manifest itself, the statutory release test is unlikely to be met.

- Where the prisoner would pose a more than minimal risk of serious harm to the public following automatic release (either at CRD or SED) but not in the period between the panel's decision to release and automatic release, and where their early release would not in any way increase the risk of harm to the public following automatic release, it could not be said that continuing detention in the period between the decision and automatic release would be "necessary for the protection of the public".

In considering risk beyond the Conditional Release date (CRD) and the Sentence Expiry date (SED) the panel may wish to seek the views of professional witnesses on the nature and likely level of risk over the longer term.

The panel must then go on to make its own assessment of risk and, in doing so, determine whether release would cause a more than minimal risk of serious harm to the public at any time. The panel will recognise, of course, that any standard or additional licence conditions will only apply for the duration of the remaining licence period, they will not apply, and therefore cannot be enforced following licence expiry.

Practitioners should remember that there are a number of preventive orders that may continue after the sentence expiry date. In sentencing, the court can impose a number of additional restrictions on serious offenders to help manage the risk of future offending, such orders are often collectively referred to as 'Ancillary Orders' and can commonly include:

- Sexual Offences Prevention Orders (SOPO) which were replaced in March 2015 by Sexual Harm Prevention orders (SHPO) s. 103A onwards of the Sexual Offences Act 2003 deals with SHPOs;

- Serious Crime Prevention orders (SCPO) which can be made on application by the Director of Public Prosecutions or the Director of the Serious Fraud Office;

- Slavery and Trafficking Prevention orders (see s. 33 of the Criminal Justice and Police Act 2001).

Again, please be advised that this list is not exhaustive and practitioners are advised to refer to the Crown Prosecution Service published legal guidance on ancillary orders if other, less common orders are referred to within the sentencing remarks or additional reports.

CHAPTER FOUR

THE PAROLE BOARD REVIEW PROCESS

The Secretary of State has set out extensive guidance in the Generic Parole Process Policy Framework which explains the roles and responsibilities of the various stakeholders involved in the parole process. It is an incredibly lengthy document and will not be set out in detail here. Instead, key aspects will be referenced to enable a thorough understanding of the parole process.

Parole reviews will start 6 months prior to the Parole Eligibility Date for prisoners serving a relevant determinate sentence and 6 months prior to tariff expiry.

For determinate sentence prisoners, further reviews will depend on the type of sentence that is being served.

For indeterminate sentence prisoners who are not released at tariff expiry, further post-tariff reviews will be held at least every 2 years.

The Parole process is often described as a two-stage process. This is because every case firstly gets considered by a Parole Board on the papers. Once a referral is made to the Board by the Secretary of State a dossier of papers is prepared and sent to the Board, this is commonly known as the Member Case Assessment (MCA) stage.

Terms of the referral

The type of sentence being served impacts on the extent of the referral. Some cases only permit the Board to consider release or remain in closed whereas some ask the Board to consider whether to make a recommendation for open conditions.

The dossier

The parole dossier will include a number of mandatory reports (these are set out within the schedule to the Parole Board Rules 2019) including, but not limited to, the Judge's sentencing remarks, any pre-sentence report, expert reports placed before the Judge at the point of sentencing, a list of previous convictions, list of prison locations, expert reports completed during the sentence, a report from the Prison Offender Manager and a report from the Community Offender Manager.

The Public Protection Casework Section (PPCS) is responsible for collating the Secretary of State's evidence and formally referring the case to the Parole Board. Dossiers are now available to practitioners via the Public Protection Unit Database (PPUD). This is an online system which covers all parole and recall cases and is operated on behalf of the National Offender Management Service (NOMS). Practitioners must register for access to PPUD.

PPUD allows access to the dossier in real time

If the Parole Board believes the dossier is incomplete it is entitled to reject the dossier and request PPCS rectifies the position.

MCA Stage

Once the parole dossier is complete the prisoner must be provided with a copy. This does not always happen so it is important to be alive to the fact that as the legal representative you may need to provide you client with a copy of the dossier or make contact with PPCS/the prison to ensure your client is provided with a paper copy.

The prisoner and the legal representative are entitled to submit representations to the Parole Board for consideration. The Parole Board allows 28 days to provide representations. This can be extended upon an application to the Parole Board but the basis for the extension will need to be properly reasoned for a Parole Board member or Parole Board Case Manager to consider. The Parole Board is increasingly making use of delegated authority for administrative matters to be consider by Parole Board Case Managers.

Drafting representations

In submitting representations to the Parole Board, we believe it is not helpful to simply rehash the facts of the case unless of course the facts are disputed. Equally you do not want to simply set out a prisoner's life history unless it has a direct bearing on the review.

Our experience is that is better to aim for short and focussed representations. Typically, representations will focus on:

i. The nature of the application;

ii. What the prisoner wants to tell the Board;

iii. Evidence of risk reduction;

iv. Applicable law;

v. If seeking an oral hearing, relevant directions etc.

It is important to remember that your representations are often the first opportunity for the prisoner's voice to be heard. You will often be asked to deal with any negative issues arising from the reports in the dossier and provide your client's explanation for any harmful behaviour, offer appropriate mitigation and challenge any apparent inaccuracies.

Ordinarily, representations will seek release on the papers or request an oral hearing before the Board.

It is important to say everything you want to say and properly reason your submissions so as to assist the member in reviewing the case but also to protect your client's position should there be a legal basis to challenge any decision taken by the Board.

If key reports are missing then guidance suggests the member should adjourn or defer the parole review to obtain the information.

Capacity

Statistics show that we have an ageing prison population, driven largely by increased numbers of older adults being convicted/sentenced for sexual offences. Additionally, there have been significant increases in the length of sentences being handed down in the courts and, consequently, we are seeing more and more people growing old in prison. This can be challenging for prison lawyers and we are now frequently dealing with clients who have impaired capacity as a result of dementia.

Furthermore, we are seeing increased numbers of mentally ill/disordered offenders being sent to prison because of the limited specialist mental health services available in the community. We are seeing increased numbers of prisoners with mental health issues and, consequently, we have to regularly consider whether our clients have the capacity to instruct us and whether we can accept and act on their instructions.

Please remember that, as practitioners, we have a professional duty under the SRA code of conduct (see 3.4) to satisfy ourselves that our client has the capacity to give instructions (see also RP v Nottingham City Council and Official Solicitor [2008] EWCA Civ 4).

Section 2(1) of the Mental Capacity Act 2005 provides that a person will not have capacity if:

1. *they cannot:*
    - *understand information relevant to the decision; or*
    - *retain that information; or*
    - *use or weigh that information as part of the process of making the decision; or*
    - *communicate the decision (by any means); and*
2. *their inability to do so is because of an impairment or disturbance in the functioning in the person's mind or brain*

The Parole Board has produced detailed and helpful guidance covering this issue and we would encourage practitioners to read and consider this carefully if you have any concerns as to whether your client(s) have capacity (see Mental Capacity Assessments and Litigation Friends Member Guidance October 2021 v 1.0)

In terms of who can identify whether a prisoner has capacity, the guidance outlines a broad list of individuals including family and friends, prison and probation staff, medical professionals as well as legal representatives. In light of this, if you are not satisfied that your client has capacity to instruct you, then you should raise your concerns at the earliest opportunity.

The guidance rather broadly suggests that anybody can, in theory, assess capacity. However, panels are encouraged to be cautious and it is provided at para. 6.3:

> *Where there is a concern that a prisoner may lack mental capacity to participate effectively, then as a general rule, and because of the consequences of any conclusion that they lack such capacity, panels will need to be assured that the issue has been determined by a professional with appropriate expertise.*

As a general rule, it is for PPCS to consider whether a mental capacity assessment is required as outlined within the guidance.

If it is assessed that your client does not have capacity then Rule 10 (6) empowers the Parole Board to appoint a litigation friend for a prisoner who is deemed to lack capacity to effectively make decisions about and participate in parole proceedings. A solicitor cannot act in a dual capacity, as they do in Mental Health cases (R (EG) v Parole Board [2020] EWHC 1457 in June 2020).

Often a litigation friend will be a family member or close friend, however, if nobody suitable can be found then a professional advocate may need to be appointed. In R (EG) v the Parole Board (referenced above), the Court found that the Official Solicitor could act as a litigation friend as a "last resort", however, it did not comment as to how this should be put in place.

Once a litigation friend has been identified and appointed, you may then continue to conduct your client's case, acting on the instructions of the appointed litigation friend.

This process can feel slightly odd and you can often feel slightly distanced from the case. It is not uncommon for Parole Board caseworkers and even the panel themselves to ask for your views/comments on any issues that arise prior to the appointment of a litigation friend. If this happens, it is important that you consider your position very carefully, in line with Law

Society guidelines you should as far practicable do everything that you can to protect your client's interests, however, in doing so you should remember that you are without instructions and, as such, you should be extremely cautious. If you have any doubts as to how you should proceed, we would advise that you contact the SRA ethics helpline.

The MCA decision

The MCA Parole Board member must follow the Parole Board's Decision-Making Framework which provides a structured approach to independent professional judgement and stresses the need for analysis, consideration, reasoning, and reflection.

The MCA member has the following options open to them:

1. Adjourn or defer for further information;

2. Issue a paper decision: a positive decision for release or recommendation for progression to open conditions, or a negative decision which refuses release or re-release and/or does not recommend progression to open conditions;

3. Direct an oral hearing or send the review to an oral hearing after a case management conference or directions hearing;

4. Direct an oral hearing after a defined period of deferral for specified developments or assessments to take place.

The general approach of the Parole Board is not to adjourn or deferral for a period exceeding four months from the date of the panel unless there are exceptional circumstances.

In considering the case the Parole Board MCA member will consider the following as part of their assessment:

Offending behaviour (the past):

i. the prisoner's history, life circumstances, age and any unique or protected characteristics (such as mental health) which should provide some context to the type/details of the offence;

ii. Any associated patterns of behaviour and their impact on others as well as any further allegations of harmful or risky behaviours either in custody of in the community.

iii. This evidence can be taken from, for example, the pre-sentence report, the judge's sentencing remarks, police computer printouts, OASys assessments, any psychological and psychiatric reports, any witness statements, and the Community Offender Manager (COM) reports. The reports may contain the prisoner's version of events as told to the report writer. Any reports of previous offending should not be relied upon exclusively unless verified elsewhere

iv. Victim Personal Statements (VPS) may be part of the dossier, although these should not provide evidence relating to risk (should the VPS provide evidence that may relate to risk, please refer to the guidance on handling the VPS to consider how this should be dealt with.

Evidence of change (the present):

v. Behaviour in custody, adjudications, security reports and drug tests, engagement with interventions, educational and vocational achievements;

vi. Evidence of the application of new skills, responses to challenges and opportunities;

vii. Recommendations for further treatment and training;

viii. In recall cases the MCA member will consider behaviour on licence, the circumstances of recall;

ix. Current risk factors and protective factors, motivation, and attitudes to offending, insight and maturity, risk assessments, and the opinions of key report writers;

x. Also, time spent in open conditions and conduct during periods of temporary release. Evidence can be found, for example, in the documentation already outlined and especially post-programme review reports, OASys assessments, security summaries, and the Prison and Community Offender Manager reports;

Manageability of risk (the future):

xi. Changes in risk factors and risk assessment scores, risk management or release plans, licence conditions and other controls, individual plans and characteristics, openness and honesty, likelihood of compliance, supportive relationships, outlook, and self-identity.

To issue a paper decision for release, the statutory test must be satisfied. Currently, the test for release is expressly laid down within the Legal Aid, Sentencing and Punishment of Offenders Act 2012 ('LASPO 2012'): "The Board must not give a direction [for release] unless the Board is satisfied that it is no longer necessary for the protection of the public that the prisoner should be confined [in prison]."

The test applies to both initial release and recall cases and to determinate sentence and indeterminate sentence prisoners. However, a recalled extended sentence prisoner who is in the "extension period" part of the sentence, must be given a presumption in favour of release. In such cases, the panel should direct release unless positively satisfied that continued detention is necessary for the protection of the public. This presumption does not apply in

In our experience Parole Board members are increasingly reluctant to release on the papers and prefer instead to direct an oral hearing to allow for evidence to be taken from the relevant witnesses.

The Board's own guidance urges MCA members to be cautious and suggests that it is more appropriate to direct an oral hearing, if the any of following apply:

- If risk assessments are finely balanced, oral evidence is likely to be helpful;
- If there is any dispute of fact or a finding of fact needs to be made;
- If key report writers have made conflicting risk assessments;
- If there are any key issues which are not addressed in reports: sometimes these may be identified by representations;
- If a case is complex or unusually serious and the member has concerns about directing release that require further exploration.

If the MCA member directs the case to an oral hearing they will set a time estimate for the hearing, list the witnesses who are required to attend to give evidence and why, set directions in order to obtain further information or reports and indicate how many Board members are required to sit on the hearing.

Issues relating to victims

The Parole Board is required to take into account any Victim Impact Statement(s) included within the dossier. If there is clear evidence to suggest that the victim(s) are engaged in the scheme, but no such statements are included within the dossier Parole Board, the guidance indicates the Board should make further enquiries.

On 4th November 2020 the Prisoners (Disclosure of Information About Victims) Act more widely known as "Helen's Law" passed into law. It came into force on 4th January 2021 and applies to all prisoners who can be released under the Crime (Sentences) Act 1997 and who are serving a sentence for murder or manslaughter; or the Criminal Justice Act 2003 for manslaughter or the taking or making of indecent images.

The Act places a statutory duty on the Parole Board to consider the non-disclosure of information about victims in its decision-making. The duty applies to cases involving the non-disclosure of information about the whereabouts of a victim's remains and non-disclosure of information about the identity of child victims in any indecent images or video recordings.

The act does not apply to recall cases whereby the Board is considering the re-release of a prisoner.

At MCA stage the Parole Board will need to consider the prisoner's non-disclosure and the reasons for the prisoner's failure to disclose the information. This will, of course, be a particular issue for prisoners who maintain their innocence.

You can see how the Parole Board deals with Helen's law in practice by reviewing one or more of the parole hearing decisions published following public hearings, as we know that Helen's law was applicable, in at least one of these decisions.

CHAPTER FIVE

HEARINGS

Automatic entitlement to an oral hearing

The following are automatically granted an oral hearing:

- Prisoners who are under the age of 18 at the point of referral (child cases): if not released on the papers, Parole Board policy is to automatically grant an oral hearing with the case prioritised in the next listing schedule.

- Prisoners in a secure hospital or mental health setting: if not released on the papers, Parole Board policy is to automatically grant an oral hearing with the case prioritised in the next listing schedule

- Prisoners facing their first review after having been in a mental health unit or secure mental health setting: if not released on the papers, Parole Board policy is to automatically grant an oral hearing with the case prioritised in the next listing schedule.

- Parole Board policy is also that there is a presumption of an oral hearing, for prisoners aged inclusively 18–21 at the point of referral (young adult cases) if they cannot be released on the papers.

Request for an oral hearing

If the Parole Board makes a no release decision on the papers, the decision is provisional for 28 days. This is because in accordance with rule 20 the prisoner has 28 days to request an oral hearing. The 28-day time limit commences from the date the decision is provided to the parties by the Parole Board.

The rationale for seeking an oral hearing can often be fact specific but the law is clear that the prospects of success in terms of a release application is not a primary consideration.

The leading case concerning oral hearings and the circumstances in which the Board is required to hold one is the Supreme Court judgment in R (Osborn, Booth and Reilly) v the Parole Board for England and Wales [2013] UKSC 61. This judgment was handed down on 9th October 2013 and the Board accepted that the judgement had wide-reaching implications.

The Supreme Court made it clear that an oral hearing should not be refused due to lack of resources, that oral hearings are not all or nothing and emphasised the fact that an oral hearing is not linked to prospects of a successful outcome.

The Supreme Court set out a non-exhaustive list of points that the Parole Board must take into account and give weight to in order to ensure procedural fairness:

- *"...the avoidance of the sense of injustice which the person who is the subject of the decision will otherwise feel...justice is intuitively understood to require a procedure which pays due respect to persons whose rights are significantly affected by decisions taken in the exercise of administrative or judicial functions..."*

- *"…the feelings of resentment that will be aroused if a party to legal proceedings is placed in a position where it is impossible for him to influence the result…"*

- Lord Reed pointed to the research carried out in the prison context by barrister and academic Nicola Padfield; this had detailed ([70]): *"…the importance attached by prisoners to a process of risk assessment which provides for their contribution to the process [and] reveals the frustration, anger and despair felt by prisoners who perceive the board's procedures as unfair, and the impact of those feelings upon their motivation and respect for authority…"*

- Lord Reed pointed to one of the board's own members (ibid) *"I find the oral hearings particularly rewarding in that the evidence of the day can sometimes illuminate a situation sufficiently to turn around my preliminary view of the case. There is no substitute for being able to hear from, and ask questions of the prisoner"*.

- "Bearing in mind however that continued detention of a post-tariff prisoner must be justified by his continuing dangerousness as independently assessed by the board, and taking account of the importance of what is at stake, it will in most cases be necessary as a matter of fairness that he should have an opportunity to appear in person before the Board".

- *"If the representations...raise issues which place in question anything in the provisional decision which may in practice have a significant impact on the prisoner's future management in prison or on his future reviews, such as reports of poor behaviour or recommendations that particular courses should be undertaken to reduce risk, it will usually follow that an oral hearing should be allowed for that reason alone, even if there*

> *is no doubt that the prisoner should remain in custody or in closed conditions".*

More recently, the courts have echoed the principles in Osborn.

In Somers vs The Parole Board [2023] EWHC 1160 (Admin) the High Court reiterated the principles in Osborn are to be applied. Where the prisoner is a post tariff lifer the case has particular protections that must be considered. The High Court in Somers went on to make clear:

- It is wrong to decline an oral hearing on the basis that there may have been little change or that the same decision might be reached after an oral hearing. The mere lack of specific recommendations relating to parole is not sufficient reason to conclude no hearing will be necessary. Osborn makes plain the value of a hearing in itself for a person in the position of a post-tariff lifer.

- This is in addition to the practical case for examining challenges to the factual evidence in the reports or exploring reports.

- New material ought to be explored when the experts provide it, particularly in the context of a post tariff prisoner, otherwise progress may go unremarked or unexplored, which would be unfair given the pressure on a prisoner to demonstrate change, development and insight when on a sentence dependent upon the Board for its duration.

- Insight, critical to progress in the criminal justice system, is by far best explored in the open forum of a hearing. The experience and expertise of the Board is second to none in understanding and exploring issues of this nature and their judgement is best exercised in the context of a hearing where they can see and assess the individual and progress or otherwise can be recorded, or indeed acted upon.

- It was wrong that the unlikelihood of release conditioned refusal of an oral hearing. These are exactly the kinds of matters covered in Osborn (relevant extract above).

- The need for a hearing to satisfy the entitlement of a prisoner to a fair consideration of his position is the stronger in the case of a post-tariff lifer and the omission to consider this aspect properly or at all is a serious omission by the Board.

- The obligation to consider the prisoner's position falls upon the Board, it is not dependent upon the prisoner, and it does, as the court in Osborn recognised, engage Article 5(4).

- It is not the case that "*if nothing could relevantly be said on behalf of the prisoner that could make a difference*" fairness does not require a hearing (see *Osborn*).

- The appropriate approach is through the lens of the common law – this generally results in Article 5(4) compliance (*Osborn).* In any event, whether or not the Claimant makes an application to be released or states an intention one way or the other the Defendant has a statutory duty to make a decision as to suitability for release necessarily therefore Article 5(4) is engaged. The likelihood of a release is not relevant when assessing whether or not to hold an oral hearing. *Osborn* indicates [112] a predisposition towards an oral hearing for indeterminate post-tariff prisoners.

The approach in Somers has been more recently reaffirmed by the High Court in McKilligan v Parole Board for England and Wales [2024] EWHC 336 (Admin). The Judge in McKilligan reiterated the following passages from Somers:

> "54. The need for a hearing to satisfy the entitlement of a prisoner to a fair consideration of his position is the stronger

> in the case of a post-tariff lifer and the omission to consider this aspect properly or at all is a serious omission by the board.
>
> 55... in my judgement the reasoning in *Osborn*, which adverts particularly to the position of the post-tariff lifer, is tantamount to articulating a presumption in favour of a hearing in such cases. Put otherwise, a good reason for not holding a hearing should be present when refusal is made in the case of a post tariff life, for whom the issues of insight, behaviour and risk (at least) are central to progress, and are almost certainly best examined and understood in the open forum of an oral hearing. The obligation to consider the prisoner's position falls upon the Board, it is not dependent upon the prisoner, and it does, as the court in *Osborn* recognised, engage article 5(4)."

If an oral hearing request is submitted to the Parole Board a duty member considers whether or not to grant an oral hearing.

If no rule 20 application for an oral hearing has been made within the 28 day timeframe the decision becomes final. Although, if the decision is eligible for reconsideration then the decision remains provisional for a further 21 days and a reconsideration application can be made at this point. If no application for reconsideration is made within the 21day time frame, the decision becomes final. We will explain the reconsideration process in more depth later.

The members of the Parole Board from our experience can sometimes fail to properly engage with why an oral hearing is required. Quite often the following standard paragraph contained within the Parole Board's Member Case Assessment Guidance is included within the decision without any evidence of meaningful engagement with the representations::

> *"The panel has considered the principles set out in the case of Osborn, Booth and Reilly (2013) UKSC 61 concerning oral hearings. It has not found that there are any reasons to hold an oral hearing. [but note whether any representations have been submitted]. Therefore, this case is not being directed to an oral hearing."*

ORAL HEARINGS

A hearing date is never set at the MCA stage. Hearing dates are considered separately by the listings team. The Board bulk lists cases each month taking into a number of factors including, amongst other things, witness availability, number of panel chairs available, number of specialist members available, and availability of a room(s) within the prison.

A hearing provides the opportunity to take oral evidence and to test evidence in support of an independent assessment of risk of serious harm and its manageability in the community. It can also be an opportunity for a prisoner to talk directly to parole decision-makers.

The Oral Hearing Guidance provides detailed best practice information covering the administration and conduct of oral hearings, including:

- The roles and responsibilities of those involved in a hearing;
- Pre-hearing practice;
- Practicalities on the day of the hearing;
- Conduct of the hearing itself; and
- The panel's decision and the timeframe in which this should be issued.

An oral hearing should not be a simply rehash each and every detail contained within the dossier. Indeed, this would be both unnecessary and time consuming, particularly given that the Parole Board often has lengthy dossiers and the material within is often clear.

The oral hearing should be a focused examination of matters that concern the panel and go to the test for release. The focus should obviously be on risk. There has been a tendency in recent years for many oral hearings to become lengthy and unfocused but there has been a deliberate attempt by the Board to ensure hearings are focused only on the issues that go to the above. Plainly this move is much welcomed by practitioners.

Generally, a panel in an oral hearing will want to address the following:

- Whether all core risk reduction has been completed?
- The extent to which the prisoner has addressed risk?
- Whether there is said to be any risk reduction/treatment outstanding?
- If there are allegations, a determination will likely be made as to the weight to be given to them, so information will be sought as to nature of the allegation?
- Whether there is any security intelligence which suggests risk is on-going?
- Whether there has been any offence parallelling behaviour?
- The prisoner's level of insight, understanding of risk and risk factors?
- The extent of the risk management plan

A panel is normally comprised of between one and three members, though very occasionally a fourth member is added. The starting point for all hearings is a single non-specialist member. Single member panels are common for determinate sentence recall hearings.

The composition of the panel at an oral hearing varies depending on the type of case and complexity of it. The MCA member can direct a specialist member, which comprises a Psychiatrist/Psychologist member of the Board to sit on a case.

A single member panel would plainly not be appropriate if a specialist member was required, where the case is so finely balanced that a single member may find it difficult to reach a decision or if there are a number of witnesses to question. Practitioners should be alive to the issues in each case and not be afraid to address any such issues in their MCA representations or to ask for pre-hearing directions to make requests considered necessary.

Following a case being directed to an oral hearing a prisoner can be expected to wait as a minimum m three months for an oral hearing. At the time of writing, it is common for a prisoner to wait for more than 6 months for their hearing to be convened. In fairness to the Parole Board, they acknowledge that there is a backlog and is appears to be taking steps to reduce this.

It is possible for an oral hearing to be prioritised or expedited and the Board has specifically published guidance for such requests. Ordinarily, cases will not be granted such status as to do so would impact on other prisoners having a timely hearing. The Board generally does not tend to grant prioritisation or expedition lightly.

The only cases that receive prioritisation as of standard at MCA stage are prisoners who are in a mental health unit, it is the prisoner's first review after discharge from a Mental Health Review Tribunal or the prisoner is under 18 years old.

Prioritisation means the listings team will take every effort to list the case within the next listings exercise. Prioritisation examples include serious concerns over the prisoners mental health or the case has been significantly delayed with a number of deferrals/adjournments.

Expedition means the listings team will take every effort to list the case as soon as possible, which includes the Board considering whether a panel can be obtained at short notice. Expedition examples include a successful reconsideration challenge or Judicial Review challenge, terminal illness of prisoner or close family member.

Due the backlogs within the Board there is a general policy that determinate sentence prisoners with less than 26 weeks [6 months] until the sentence expiry date or automatic release date will not usually be directed to an oral hearing because the Board struggles to provide a hearing within this timeframe. If reasons exist why an expedited hearing should take place then an oral hearing may be possible.

A party who wishes to make representations to the Board in respect of the oral hearing e.g. submissions from the prisoner must in accordance with rule 18 provide it no less than 14 days before the hearing. This includes material in which the prisoner wishes to rely upon.

Case management conferences and directions hearings

From our experience case management conferences and directions hearings are often an extremely valuable for practitioners in aiming to ensure that in due course an effective oral hearing can take place. Rule 7 of the Parole Board rules covers case conferences and directions hearings.

A case conference is supposed to be short, light touch approach discussion usually staged by teleconference or video-link via MS Teams, to try to resolve any identified issues. A case management conference cannot formally take evidence.

Ordinarily case management conferences and directions hearings are for relatively complex cases which have specific features for which such a hearing is necessary. It may be because specialist expert reports are required, if there has been issues of non-compliance with directions, the capacity and litigation friend guidance is to be applied or if the case has been granted a public parole hearing and there is a need to discuss logistics.

Either party to the proceedings (PPCS or the prisoner/prisoner's representative) may request a case management conference by submitting a Stakeholder Response Form (SHRF) to the Parole Board case manager. Each party will be given the opportunity to submit representations to be considered by the MCA panel. All representations must be submitted within 7 days of being informed of the request to avoid delay. The final decision as to whether a case management conference is required rests with MCA panel. Where the MCA panel accepts the request for a case management conference, or directs that one is held, they will be the panel responsible for chairing it. If the MCA panel direct the case to an oral hearing and assess that the case may benefit from a case management conference, they can suggest this when making the direction to an oral hearing but should not direct it. It will be for the panel chair allocated to the oral hearing to decide whether one is needed.

A directions hearing can be directed for the purpose of unpicking a complex matter, seek clarification from a range of witnesses, or establish other facts as part of the MCA process. A directions hearing may be required in order for the MCA panel to determine how to proceed with a case prior to making the MCA decision/directions.

Directions hearings can be particularly helpful in cases where there is multi-agency involvement, such as cases involving mental health issues or where there is a prospect of release needing specialised funded accommodation or a wider care package. The parties in attendance may include the prisoner and representative, officials including the COM and Prison Offender Managers (POM), and potentially a PPCS Secretary of

State Representative. Other participants may be directed to attend as necessary to discuss directions.

The directions will confirm which participants should take part in the directions hearing. The prisoner need not attend but should be offered the opportunity. The representative must be involved (unless they have made it clear that they do not wish to attend) and the Secretary of State (via PPCS) must be offered the opportunity to attend.

Where the MCA panel requires a directions hearing to be held in order to make a decision on the progression of the case, they will be the panel responsible for chairing it. If the MCA panel direct the case to an oral hearing and assess that the case may benefit from a directions hearing, they can suggest this but should not direct it. It will be for the panel chair allocated to the oral hearing to decide whether one is required.

A directions hearing does not allow the MCA panel to take evidence. The nature of future evidence can be discussed but evidence should not be formally taken.

Case conferences and directions hearings should be audibly recorded.

Specialist panel members

If a member directs a case to an oral hearing they will need to consider whether there is a need for a specialist member to be part of the oral hearing panel. A specialist member is either a psychiatrist or psychologist. Careful consideration is required because they are in short supply. The member will need to consider whether to simply specify that a specialist member is required or specifically state psychiatrist or psychologist. At MCA stage this is something that you can consider as part of the representation process.

Being non-specific may be appropriate when:

- There are mental health concerns or evidence of psychological distress with an identified or suggested link to the prisoner's risk of reoffending or harm, e.g., substance misuse, anxiety, depression or self-esteem issues, but these have not been such as to require transfer to hospital for treatment during the sentence nor does follow up mental health care need to be arranged ahead of release.

- Personality disorder or psychopathy has been identified or suggested and the Offender Personality Disorder Pathway will contribute to future management.

- There is a learning disability, developmental disorder/neurodiversity e.g., autism, Asperger's Syndrome, attention deficit hyperactivity disorder (ADHD) or brain injury.

- The case has complex or serious risks issues, e.g. the prisoner has exhibited a range of offending behaviour, offending involves multiple victim types or sadistic behaviour, motivation for the offence(s) is unclear and the prisoner denies some or all aspects of their offence.

As a starting point, Parole Board members should have a reasonable understanding of ant psychological evidence given they are considered experts in risk assessment and will likely have reviewed psychological formulations in the past. Generally, a psychologist member would not be added to a panel simply because there are psychological assessments contained within the dossier. The Board's guidance suggests a psychologist member may be appropriate if there are two or more differing psychological opinions e.g., a Prison Service psychological report and an external psychological report or if the issues are complex e.g. psychopathy, personality disorder or learning difficulties.

Psychiatrist members from the Board are in significant demand and the Board will reserve such members for cases where the prisoner has an obvious major mental illness such as schizophrenia, if they have previously been detained in hospital, if they have dementia or where are other concerns around capacity.

Requests for additional witnesses and/or observers

Rules 13 and 14 covers Witnesses and Observers. Rule 13 makes it clear that a request to call a witness at an oral hearing must be made within a written application no later than 12 weeks before the date of the oral hearing. The time limit is the same for observers under rule 14.

From experience requests made by PPCS/SSJ are not particularly well reasoned and typically observer requests do not make mention of whether permission has been sought from the prisoner. Generally, as a matter of good practice, the prisoner (who is of course the focus of the review) should be asked to confirm if they are agreeable.

A common issue for practitioners is that often witness and observer requests on behalf of prisoners are raised shortly before the hearing. In such circumstances an application will need to be made to the Board relying on rule 9 which allows a duty member or panel chair to amend the time limits for any rule. A full explanation as to why the application has not been made in accordance with the rules should be set out.

If the request has been made by another party, Practitioners should respond in robust terms to ensure that they have sufficient time to take instructions from their client.

Victim attendance and/or participation

Victims are entitled through the victim liaison scheme to have involvement in a parole review. They can submit a victim impact statement and, if they so wish, attend the hearing and read it out to the panel. The Parole Board adopts a policy whereby there is a presumption that any requests from a victim to read their statement to the oral hearing panel will be agreed. If they do not wish to read it personally then someone else is able to read it on their behalf. It is best practice for victim impact statements to be submitted in advance of the MCA review, but most commonly they are not received until in the run up to an oral hearing. A prisoner is not mandated to be present when a victim impact statement is read and it is worth discussing with the prisoner before any oral hearing as to what they wish to do. In some cases it can impact on achieving best evidence for a prisoner to listen to the statement immediately before the parole hearing.

Non-Disclosure

Rule 17 provides the mechanism for non-disclosure. Non-disclosure effectively means there is a mechanism to withhold certain information from a prisoner and in limited circumstances also from his/her legal representative.

The general starting point is that all material to be considered by the Parole Board should be disclosed to the prisoner as they have a right to know what the case against them is. This fits with procedural fairness as the prisoner must be able to respond to the case against them.

If material is to be withheld it is important then it is important that steps are taken to ensure that your client is sufficiently able to consider the material and respond to it. In many instances the Parole Board will direct that a gist of the material is provided to the prisoner. This 'gist' should be a summary of the material(s) that is the subject of the non disclosure application and should give the prisoner sufficient information to respond to it and refute it if necessary.

The Board ideally should be flexible in its approach to strike an appropriate balance.

Rule 17 allows the Secretary of State for Justice or a third party authorised by the SSJ to apply to the Board for information or report to be withheld from a prisoner and/or representative. Most commonly non-disclosure material encompasses prison security intelligence/victim impact statements. The Board has issued guidance to its members and outlined the following examples:

- a victim does not wish a prisoner to see their VPS as they will be adversely affected by the very fact of disclosure, over and above the distress already caused by the offence and the forthcoming Parole Board hearing. The VPS form will include contextual information behind a request for non-disclosure.

- disclosure of the material could compromise the safety of its source. In some cases, this will not prevent disclosure of sufficient detail to the prisoner to know the case against them. However, in others it may be very difficult indeed, especially when the information to be withheld contains the key details that would be necessary for the prisoner to challenge it.

- disclosure of the material could compromise intelligence-gathering methods and enable the prisoner or others to shape their practices to avoid detection.

- the prisoner themself is a source (sometimes called a Covert Human Intelligence Source or CHIS11). In these circumstances, of course, the prisoner is well aware of what they have told the authorities but understandably do not wish it to become known to others (even, sometimes, their own representative) through having it mentioned in the dossier.

- disclosure of the information might jeopardise ongoing operations, either to gather intelligence or to disrupt criminal activities. In such a case, the panel member will need to remember that the potential wider damage that might occur if the ongoing operations were so disrupted can be a valid reason to withhold material, as long as it can be done so in a way that is necessary and proportionate.

- the owner of the information, who may be a third party such as the police or another information owner, is unwilling to declassify information that they have provided so that it can move into open 10 In some instances, information may come up in the period shortly prior to an Oral Hearing, or on the day of the Oral Hearing that relates to non-disclosure – please see section 12.6 onwards for more information.

The grounds for making such requests are limited to material in which the disclosure would adversely affect:

a. national security;

b. the prevention of disorder or crime, or

c. the health or welfare of the prisoner or any other person, and

d. that withholding the material is a necessary and proportionate measure in the circumstances of the case.

Rule 17 is clear that such applications should be made no later than 8 weeks before the oral hearing date, but in practice the SSJ does not seemingly respect this rule that they themselves introduced and it is not uncommon for such applications to be a few weeks or even days before the hearing. Late applications place the Board and prisoner in an extremely difficult position because the Parole Board does not often proceed with a hearing when there are unresolved non-disclosure applications due to the potential for that information to be relevant to their risk assessment. In these circumstances the Board tend to utilise rule 9 and extend the time.

Whether or not it is appropriate to extend the time limit under rule 9 will depend on all the circumstances of the case and in particular:

a. whether there is an acceptable reason for the failure to comply with rule 17(2); and

b. whether extending the time limit or declining to do so would result in any (and if so what) unfairness to either party.

Member guidance considers fairness in such circumstances and considers whether:

a. Extending the time limit will not normally be fair to the prisoner if the application is made so close to the hearing date that it is likely to result in an adjournment of the hearing;

b. Declining to extend the time limit may be unfair to the Secretary of State (and potentially also to the prisoner and wider public protection) if it is likely to result in relevant material being excluded from the panel's consideration.

c. Many non-disclosure applications relate to a VPS. Where that is the case, consideration needs to be given to the anxiety and distress which a victim may be feeling when engaging in the process and the challenges that may be faced in meeting deadlines.

The party making the application to the Board must provide the Parole Board with the material and a written application as to why the material meets one of the limbs of the test for non-disclosure.

A Parole Board member either a duty member or panel chair will then review the application and direct one of the following, that the material should be;

(a) served on the prisoner and their representative (if applicable) in full;

(b) withheld from the prisoner or from both the prisoner and their representative, or

(c) disclosed to the prisoner, or to both the prisoner and the prisoner's representative (if applicable) in the form of a summary or redacted version.

If the Board directs the material should be served on the prisoner and the representative in full the rules permit the SSJ to appeal the decision.

The Rules require the SSJ must notify the prisoner and the representation as practicable once a non-disclosure application is made. Some case managers are excellent at informing representatives that a non-disclosure application has been submitted. Others don't inform in advance and often the first time we become aware of it is once the Board has made a decision.

If material is to be withheld from the prisoner and their representative then Rule 14 (8) allows the appointment of a special advocate. Rule 14 (8) the panel chair or duty member can direct the appointment of a special advocate. The Attorney General has a panel of practising barristers who can act as a special advocate. Ordinarily, a list of barristers is provided to the legal representative who can in consultation with the prisoner set out which barrister they would wish to be appointed. This process is designed to ensure the prisoners rights are sufficiently protected as the special advocate then deals with the material on the prisoners behalf.

If the representative is to receive non-disclosure but the prisoner is not permitted to receive it then the SSJ will ordinarily ask the representative to give an undertaking that it will not be disclosed to the prisoner. An undertaking allows the legal representative to receive the material to deal with it on the prisoner's behalf.

If the Board considers an appeal then the rules specify the appeal is decided by the Chair of the Parole Board. However, in practice this is delegated to a small cohort of members of the Board. An appeal can be submitted by either the prisoner or the SSJ.

Occasionally, the non-disclosure material may have a specific security classification which means it must be stored in secure conditions and cannot be shared outside those conditions. This is rare, but in such circumstances the Parole Board and PPCS will set up a 'revelation meeting'. This is an opportunity for the panel member to attend a meeting in a secure environment where the closed material will be shown to them. PPCS officials and members of the secretariat with appropriate clearance may be present, and it is possible for third parties such as the police to also be there to assist PPCS in presenting the material. The revelation meeting is not a hearing or an opportunity for the Secretary of State to argue their case: it is so that the panel member can view the closed material and ask any questions that they have about its content in order to make a decision about how to progress the application.

Remote hearings

Pre-Covid the majority of hearings were face-to-face, however, the pandemic required the Board to conduct hearings remotely.

Our initial concerns as to whether remote hearings would have an impact on the release rate of the Board appear to have been misplaced and the data has confirmed that remote hearings have not had any particular impact in this regard.

Having experienced remote hearings now for several years they are generally considered to be extremely effective. The Parole Board are now experienced in conducting hearings remotely and they have very much become the norm. The Board's starting point is now that a hearing will be considered suitable for a remote hearing, unless there is a particular feature of the case, which necessitates a face-to-face hearing. In determining whether a face to face hearing is required the Board will consider factors, which include:

- The health of the prisoner e.g. physical or mental health which suggests fairness requires a face-to-face hearing;

- Complex risk assessments;

- The prisoner is under the age 18;

- Language issues;

It is now quite common for face-to-face hearings to be listed as hybrid hearings meaning a mixture of individuals will be in person or remote. It is common in such situations for probation officers to attend remotely along with the panel. The POM and the legal representative can then attend in person at the prison.

Prisons are generally quite good at arranging pre-hearing conferences with the prisoner, but do not hesitate to make contact with the prison to ensure you have a pre-hearing conference with your client before the hearing on the day.

During the course of the hearing the panel will ensure you can speak to your client at any point. Panels are very good at ensuring prisoners and their legal representatives are able to effectively communicate during the hearing.

Time estimates

In setting the hearing estimate panels are now expected to be set out in quite some detail why they considering a hearing will take a set time breaking it down into chunks e.g. 30 minutes pre-panel discussion etc. This has seemingly assisted panels to be more focused and for the Board to ensure that there is sufficient time to have a full and effective hearing and avoid adjourning part heard.

Questioning witnesses and order of evidence

It is now generally accepted that it is for the panel to lead with the questioning of the witnesses. Many years ago it was common for legal representatives to lead with the questioning, which could be tricky as you often had to second guess areas the question would panel. It seems much more focused for a panel to question first, although if for a particular reason you consider it appropriate to lead with the questions then do not hesitate to express this to the panel.

The common order of witnesses in a parole hearing is the POM, prisoner and then COM. The legal representative's focus should be on the statutory release test and you will be surprised the number of POM's, COM's and prison psychologists who do not know the Board's statutory release test. Asking them directly can often be helpful if/when they are not supporting a prisoner for release or open conditions.

The Secretary of State (SSJ) is a part to the hearing and is entitled to be represented. It is relatively uncommon for a representative of the SSJ to attend and generally they only attend in high profile cases, terrorism (TACT) cases or cases that are otherwise considered to be noteworthy. SSJ representatives tend to be former probation officers and often do not have any formal legal training. If an SSJ representative does attend they are able to offer representations to the panel along with questioning the witnesses and prisoner.

Allegations

The Parole Board can and indeed must consider unproven allegations in the course of the review. In doing so they use the civil burden of proof, that is to say the balance of probabilities. This means the Board can properly consider criminal matters which did not result in a charge, for example where no further action (NFA) was taken.

The definition of "allegation" is contained within the Board's published Guidance on Allegations (September 2023 v 2.0) which states at paragraph 1.2:

> "*The term 'Allegation' refers to conduct alleged to have occurred which has not been adjudicated upon. Adjudications can include a finding by a criminal or a civil court or a prison adjudication*".

Allegations which are relevant are those which, if true, could affect the panel's risk analysis. Allegations may be of harmful behaviour and/or 'risky' behaviour. Sometimes these allegations are currently being investigated by the police or others and may be disposed of or adjudicated on in the future.

Once it is established that an allegation has been made, panels will need to carefully consider the allegation when making a parole decision. Fairness remains at the heart of the issue, but panel's will often wish to rigoursly pursue information and seemingly conduct mini-trials.

Understandably, the lawfulness of this approach has been thoroughly tested through the courts. The issue went through the High Court, Court of Appeal and was eventually considered by the Supreme Court in the case of Pearce.

R (on the application of Pearce and another) (Respondents) v Parole Board for England and Wales Case ID: 2022/0052

Two questions fell to be determined:

1) When the Parole Board is deciding whether or not to direct the release of a prisoner on licence, can it only take into account allegations if they are proved on the balance of probabilities?

2) Does the Parole Board's "Guidance on Allegations" (the Guidance) misstate the law on this issue?

The Supreme Court allowed the Parole Board's appeal and held that risk may be assessed without the judicial body being able to make a finding of fact(s).

Depending upon the legal context, the judicial body can assess risk by weighing up the possibility that an allegation 'may' be true having regard to the whole material before it.

The Supreme Court found no basis for the contention that fairness requires the Board to have regard only to proven facts in making its assessment.

Public hearings

Since July 2022 Parole Board hearings can be held in public if an application is made and if the Board decides to allow it. In deciding whether to allow it, the Chair of the Parole Board will consider whether it is in the interests of Justice for the hearing to be held in public.

The starting point is that hearings will remain private because it is of fundamental importance that witnesses are able to give their best evidence in an environment where an open and honest discussion can take place.

Parties can make an application to the Chair of the Parole Board for a public parole hearing. The Board has issued guidance on the issues it will consider when determining whether or not a public parole hearing is required/justified.

Practitioners should be willing/prepared to take instructions from their clients as to whether they wish to apply for a public hearing, although such applications are likely to be rare, readers will note that of the limited number of public hearings that have taken place, thus far, half of those followed requests by the prisoner themself.

More commonly, practitioners will be instructed to resist an application for a public hearing. In doing this, the focus will likely be on fairness to your client who will likely to be terrified by the prospect of a public hearing and, in particular, the prospect of discussing highly sensitive matters in front of a large audience. This prospect is likely to be extremely distressing for the majority of our clients and practitioners should be alive to this. If you have concerns that your client and other witnesses would not be able to give frank and honest evidence then you should resist an application for a public hearing. The Board's core function is to assess risk on all of the evidence before them and if witnesses are on edge and unwilling to speak in a frank/honest manner then it is prudent to argue that the panel's ability to make a fair and effective decision could be impaired.

The Parole Board publishes all application decisions whether the application was successful or rejected. There is no automatic right of appeal against the Chair's decision, but if circumstances change or new information becomes available the Chair is generally open to reconsidering the decision.

At the time of writing four public parole hearings have taken place. To provide context they have been for the following prisoners:

1) **Charles Salvador** – previously known as Charles Bronson. This was a prisoner application for a public hearing to shine a light on

his significant post tariff status and his detention within deep custody, namely the Close Supervision Centre system;

2) **Russell Causley** – This was a victim led request for a public hearing. Mr. Causley had been recalled to prison and the victim's had applied to consider how the *Prisoners (Disclosure of Information About Victims) Act* more widely known as "Helen's Law" was to be applied;

3) **Glynn Razzell** – This was another victim led request. Mr. Razzell was convicted of murder and had not disclosed the location of his wife's remains. This was another examination of how the *Prisoners (Disclosure of Information About Victims) Act* was applied;

4) **Nicholas Bidar** – This was a prisoner application. Mr. Bidar applied as a significantly post tariff IPP prisoner who had been kept as a category A prisoner. He was the first IPP to have a public parole hearing as he wanted to highlight the plight of IPP prisoners.

At the time of writing a further four applications have been accepted for a public hearing, however, they are yet to have the hearing take place. We understand that twenty-four applications have been refused a public hearing.

CHAPTER SIX

POST-HEARING

How does the panel reach its decision?

Oral hearing panel decisions are made on a majority basis in accordance with Rule 26. If a panel is unable to reach a majority decision then it becomes a split decision and it will be relisted and another panel will consider the case. This will only happen in the cases involving two panel members.

In accordance with rule 25 (6) decisions must be provided to the parties no later than 14 days following the hearing. This 14-day window includes non-working days.

Any decision issued by a panel which is eligible for reconsideration eligible is provisional and becomes final when/if no reconsideration application is made. Any decision that is not eligible for reconsideration becomes final when served on the parties.

Rule 27 of the rules enables the Parole Board to issue summaries of its decisions. The rule provides that the Board must produce a summary of its reasons for the decision unless the chair considers that exceptional circumstances exist as to why a summary should not be provided. Exceptional circumstances may include the safety of the prisoner.

Reconsideration

Rule 28 of the rules covers reconsideration. Reconsideration was introduced following a review initiated by the SSJ in response to the Board's decision to release John Worboys (see *R (DSD and NVB) v Parole*

Board of England and Wales). The reconsideration mechanism commenced in July 2019.

The reconsideration criteria are the same criteria as for Judicial Review. Parties may now apply to the Board for eligible decisions to be reconsidered where it is argued:

(a) that the decision is irrational and/or

(b) that it is procedurally unfair and/or

(c) it contains an error of law

Under Rule 28(1) of the Parole Board Rules 2019 the only kind of decision which is eligible for reconsideration is a decision that the prisoner is or is not suitable for release on licence. Such a decision is eligible for reconsideration whether it is made by a paper panel (Rule 19(1)(a) or (b)) or by an oral hearing panel after an oral hearing (Rule 25(1)) or by an oral hearing panel which makes the decision on the papers (Rule 21(7)).

Decisions are eligible for reconsideration only where a prisoner is serving:

a) An indeterminate sentence;

b) An extended sentence;

c) A determinate sentence subject to initial release by the Board under Chapter 6 Part 12 of the 2003 Act; or

d) A serious terrorism sentence (under sections 268A and 282A of the Sentencing Code).

These sentence types include:

- All types of life sentence (discretionary, mandatory or automatic);

- Imprisonment for Public Protection (IPP);
- Extended Determinate Sentences (EDS);
- Sentences for Offenders of Particular Concern (SOPC);
- Discretionary Conditional Release (DCR)
- Sentences for terrorism or terrorism-related crime to which the Terrorist Offenders (Restriction of Early Release) Act 2020 applies; and
- Old legacy extended sentences – Extended Public Protection (EPP) sentences and former 'section 85' extended sentences (ESP).

Decisions about transfer to open conditions, case management decisions, or licence variations, and decisions not to grant an oral hearing after a decision not to release has been made on the papers are not eligible for reconsideration.

Decisions are now published at the conclusion of the relevant proceedings. You can view reconsideration decisions using Bailii (bailii.org/ew/cases/PBRA)

In advising clients it is important that practitioners remember that merely being unhappy with a decision does not give grounds for reconsideration and that the threshold for applications for reconsideration is high. In truth legal test is essentially the same as the test for Judicial Review.

The Secretary of State for Justice seemingly challenges any high-profile Parole Board decision irrespective of the legal merit. An example of this is the case involving Colin Pitchfork. In this case the Board considered a dossier of over 1000 pages. The panel heard evidence from 5 professional witnesses and adjourned the hearing so further information could be received. All professional witnesses agreed there was no core risk reduction work to complete. Furthermore, all the professional witnesses had agreed the test for release was met. They were satisfied that the risk management plan (RMP) was sufficiently robust and stringent with over 30 licence conditions. As such they were agreed that the proposed RMP was capable of managing Mr. Pitchfork's risks in the community. The Judicial Member who considered the reconsideration application decided the decision reached by the panel was justified on the evidence they heard and considered and further that the decision was adequately and sufficiently explained.

Irrationality

In respect of legal irrationality, the Board routinely relies upon the case of Wells it is suggested that rather than ask "was the decision being considered irrational" the better approach is to test the decision maker's ultimate conclusions against all the evidence received and ask whether the conclusions reached can be safely justified on the basis of that evidence while giving due deference to the panel's experience and expertise.

In **R (DSD and others) v the Parole Board** [2018] **EWHC** 694 **(Admin),** the Divisional Court set out the test for irrationality to be applied in judicial reviews of Parole Board decisions. It said at para. 116,

> *"The issue is whether the release decision was so outrageous in its defiance of logic or accepted moral standards that no sensible person who had applied his mind to the question to be decided could have arrived at it."*

In Wells, R (On the Application Of) v Parole Board [2019] EWHC 2710 (Admin) adopted a modern approach to Wednesbury irrationality. Justice Saini in Wells noted:

A modern approach to the Associated Provincial Picture Houses Ltd v Wednesbury Corporation (1948) 1 KB 223 (CA) test is not to simply ask the crude and unhelpful question: was the decision irrational?

A more nuanced approach in modern public law is to test the decision-maker's ultimate conclusion against the evidence before it and to ask whether the conclusion can (with due deference and with regard to the Panel's expertise) be safely justified on the basis of that evidence, particularly in a context where anxious scrutiny needs to be applied.

I emphasise that this approach is simply another way of applying Lord Greene MR's famous dictum in Wednesbury (at 230: "no reasonable body could have come to [the decision]") but it is preferable in my view to approach the test in more practical and structured terms on the following lines: does the conclusion follow from the evidence or is there an unexplained evidential gap or leap in reasoning which fails to justify the conclusion?

Procedural Fairness

A party seeking to complain of procedural unfairness under Rule 28 has to establish that either:

(a) express procedures laid down by the law were not followed in the making of the relevant decision;

(b) they were not given a fair hearing;

(c) they were not properly informed of the case against them

(d) they were prevented from putting their case fairly; and/or

(e) the panel was not impartial.

The overriding objective is to ensure that the Applicant's case was not dealt with justly.

Error of law

This ground is much narrower in scope and, we would imagine, is rarely argued by practitioners. A decision can be challenged on this basis if the panel had, for example acted without/outside their jurisdiction.

Time limits for reconsideration

There are strict time limits for making an application for reconsideration, the application must be made within three weeks (21 calendar days) of the decision being issues to the parties in the case (the prisoner and his/her representative and the SSJ).

The initial decision will become final if there have been no applications within that 21 day window and the Board will not accept any requests made after the three week window has closed.

The Slip Rule

This common law principle applies to case before the Parole Board and is covered in rule 30. Rule 30 (1) states the Board may at any time correct an accidental slip or omission in a decision and rule 30 (2) allows a party to apply for a correction without notice.

Setting Aside

Section 133 of the Police, Crime Sentencing and Courts Act 2022 provides the Board with the power to set aside a decision in cases where the relevant criteria are met.

Rule 28 of the Parole Board Rules sets out the procedure for exercising this power. The power applies to decisions made on or after 21st July 2022. Only the parties to the proceedings (Secretary of State or the prisoner often via his/her legal representative) can make an application to set aside a final decision. The Parole Board can also apply to set aside a decision on its own initiative if the relevant criteria are met, although this will be rare.

The decision under challenge must be a final decision and relate to whether the prisoner should be released or not released. A decision regarding a recommendation for open conditions, other Parole Board advice cases or IPP licence terminations are not eligible for the set aside process.

The provision can be applied to determinate and indeterminate sentence prisoners where the relevant criteria and tests are met. In cases where the application to set aside a release decision relates to there having been an error of law or fact, the time limit for filing an application is 21 days after the decision under challenge becomes final.

The time limit for challenging a release decision on the basis of there being new information, or where there has been a change in circumstances, is any time up until the point of release but not once the prisoner has been released on licence into the community.

If the decision under challenge is a release decision, there are three grounds upon which a setting aside application can be made. These are:

a. An Error of Law or Fact: That the direction for release would not have been made but for an error of law or fact;

b. New information: That the direction for release would not have been made if information that was not available to the panel when the direction was made had been available; and/or

c. Change in circumstances: That the direction for release would not have been made if the change in circumstances relating to the prisoner had occurred before the direction was given.

Under previous parole board rules a decision was made at the point in which the panel members had agreed the point it becomes final. written decision, but it has since been changed to the point at which it is issued to the parties. At that

In *Dickins v Parole Board [2021] EWHC 1166 (Admin)* the question for the Court was when the Parole Board directs a prisoner's release at what exact point, legally, in the parole process, has the Parole Board legally given that direction? That was the legal hair that had to be split in Dickins. Is it when the chair has drafted the decision; is it when it is circulated to panel members; is it when the panel has agreed the final wording; or is it when the panel chair sends it to the case manager; is it when the case manager communicates the decision to the parties? The legal advisor to the Parole Board advised the panel that it was functus when it made its decision directing release and emailed it to the case manager, thereafter it was functus officio and had no authority to take any further action at all.

The Secretary of State then sought to have the decision to release Mr Dickins reconsidered under the Reconsideration Mechanism, and was successful, consequently the release decision was quashed.

Mr. Dickins sought to challenge that decision and, having done so, the High Court ruled that the panel were powerless to change their decision once it had been emailed to the case manager. The court referred to this as a 'hard case'.

At the point the decision is issued to the parties the Parole Board is functus. This is because it is a statutory body and its only powers are those given to it by statute. Once a decision is issued the Board it has no further power until a case is referred back to it by the Secretary of State, there is a successful reconsideration/set aside application, or a decision is quashed following a judicial review.

In some instances, the Board will be supplied with information after an oral hearing has concluded but before the decision has been made that indicates a change in circumstances, such as so-called "adverse developments". This could be a failed drug test, an adjudication or an act of violence. In such instances the parole board case manager will pass the information to the panel chair and should disclose the developments to the legal representative as submissions/representations may wish to be made. It is then open to the panel to adjourn, conclude the case or if fairness requires direct a further hearing.

If the decision has been made the Board should consider if the case is eligible to be set aside.

IPP/DPP Licence Termination

Current position

Currently IPP and DPP (people who received their IPP sentence as a child) sentenced prisoners qualify for licence termination 10 years after their first release on licence. This 10-year period is known as the 'qualifying period' and at the end of that period can apply to the Parole Board.

This can be done whether or not the prisoner has been recalled and even if the prisoner is in custody at the end of the qualifying period.

If the licence is not terminated, the case is reviewed by the Parole Board each following year.

The Future

The Victims and Prisoners Act (VAPA) was one of the last bills passed before parliament was dissolved prior to the 2024 General Election and it became law on 24th May 2024.

The VAPA is of significant importance to those serving IPP and DPP sentences. For IPP sentences the 'qualifying period' is to be reduced from ten years to three years following a prisoner's first release from custody. For those who were given a DPP sentence the period is now two years after first release. Termination reviews will be automatic and prisoners will no longer have to make an application.

The Act creates a presumption that IPP and DPP licences will be terminated, unless the Parole Board believes that there good reasons to leave it in place.

The Act also introduces what is called a 'sunset clause'. If the Parole Board decides to leave a person's IPP licence in place after the qualifying period has expired, a two year 'clock' starts. If the person avoids being recalled in that two-year period, their IPP sentence will automatically be terminated. If a person is recalled within those two years, the clock restarts upon re-release. The Act also gives the Secretary of State a new power to stop recalls counting against the sunset clause if they believe it is appropriate to do so.

People serving IPP sentences who have been recalled will be eligible for Risk Assessed Recall Reviews (RARR – formerly called executive release). This is a power of the Secretary of State to re-release people who have been recalled without them having to be referred to the Parole Board. Previously this power only applied to people serving determinate sentences.

On 5th September 2024, the SSJ announced the plans to implement the changes that will affect those serving IPP and DPP sentences and, significantly, the timeframe for those changes, some of which will be effective from 1st November 2024 with other changes to come later in February 2025.

All of the changes, save for the reduced qualifying period, will be effective from 1st November, these changes are:

- The change to the test to be applied by the Parole Board when considering termination will change meaning that there will be a presumption in favour of termination and, if the Board are not minded to terminate then they will need to show 'strong justification on public protection grounds' as to why they are so minded;

- The new executive release power allowing the SSJ to administratively release prisoners serving IPP or DPP sentences; and

- A requirement that the SSJ lays an annual report before Parliament as to the steps being taken to progress those serving IPP sentences towards being safely released.

Then from February 2025 the qualifying period for licence termination will be reduced. Those serving IPP will be automatically referred for a termination review three years after their first release (if they have not already one). For DPPs this referral will be made two years after their first release.

With the permission of UNGRIPP we are sharing this helpful flowchart which clearly details the changes that will come into force in February 2025.

These changes come into force on 1st February 2025

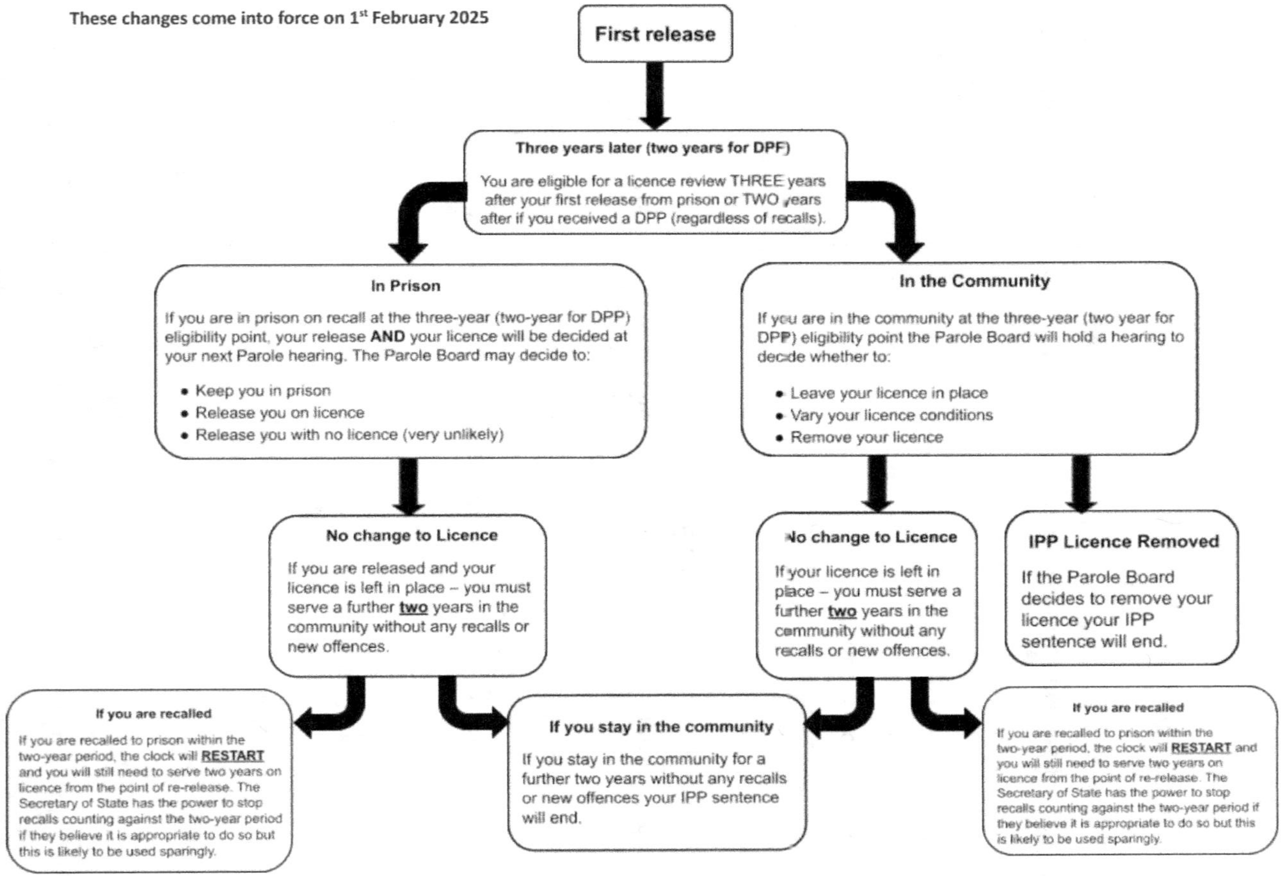

CONCLUDING REMARKS

As prison law practitioners our numbers are ever dwindling and reducing as evidenced by the research undertaken by the Association of Prison Lawyers.

The Association of Prison Lawyers are a friendly bunch with a members portal for members to post prison law related questions.

We would encourage any prison law practitioner to join the association and tap into the portal and some excellent training events.

As a last word, John and I's door is always open so if you have a particular parole related query then by all means reach out to us and we will happily assist.

We have within the accompanying appendix set out a full copy of the Parole Board Rules for your assistance.

APPENDIX

THE PAROLE BOARD RULES

STATUTORY INSTRUMENTS

2019 No. 1038

PRISONS, ENGLAND AND WALES

The Parole Board Rules 2019

Made - - - -	*20th June 2019*
Laid before Parliament	*24th June 2019*
Coming into force - -	*22nd July 2019*

The Secretary of State, in exercise of the powers conferred by sections 239(5), 330(3) and (4) of the Criminal Justice Act 2003(**a**), makes the following Rules.

PART 1

Introduction

Citation, commencement and revocation

1.—(1) These Rules may be cited as the Parole Board Rules 2019 and come into force on 22nd July 2019.

(2) The Parole Board Rules 2016(**b**) and the Parole Board (Amendment) Rules 2018(**c**) are revoked.

Interpretation

2. In these Rules—

"1997 Act" means the Crime (Sentences) Act 1997(**d**);

"2003 Act" means the Criminal Justice Act 2003;

"assessment panel" means a panel appointed under rule 5(4) to consider reconsideration applications under rule 28;

"barrister" means an individual who has been called to the Bar by an Inn of Court and holds a current practising certificate;

"Board" means the Parole Board(**e**);

"Board chair" means the chairman of the Board appointed under paragraph 2 of Schedule 19 to the 2003 Act;

"case" means any matter referred to the Board by the Secretary of State, including a request for advice;

(**a**) 2003 c. 44.
(**b**) S. I. 2016/1041.
(**c**) S. I. 2018/541.
(**d**) 1997 c. 43.
(**e**) The Parole Board is continued in existence by section 239(1) of the Criminal Justice Act 2003 (c. 44).

"custodian" means a prison officer under the Prison Act 1952(**a**), an officer of a contracted-out prison under the Criminal Justice Act 1991(**b**), or any person employed to work in a prison;

"determinate sentence" means a sentence served by a fixed-term prisoner as defined by section 237 of the 2003 Act;

"direct application" means an application made by a prisoner directly to the Board under rule 31;

"duty member" means a member of the Board appointed under rule 4(2);

"extended sentence" means an extended sentence for certain violent or sexual offences under sections 226A, 226B, 227 and 228 of the 2003 Act(**c**), or section 85 of the Powers of Criminal Courts (Sentencing) Act 2000(**d**);

"indeterminate sentence" means a sentence listed under section 34(2) of the 1997 Act;

"members of staff" means employees appointed under paragraph 5 of Schedule 19 to the 2003 Act;

"offender" means a prisoner or a person released from prison on licence;

"oral hearing" means a hearing before a panel appointed under rule 5(2);

"panel" means a panel of one or more members appointed under rule 5(1), (2), (3) or (5);

"panel chair" means the person who is chairing a panel by virtue of rule 5(6);

"party" means a prisoner or the Secretary of State;

"previous review" means the Secretary of State's previous referral of the prisoner's case to the Board relating to the prisoner's release under the 1997 Act or 2003 Act;

"prison" includes a young offender institution or any other institution where a prisoner is detained;

"prison director" means a person appointed under section 85(1)(a) of the Criminal Justice Act 1991;

"prisoner" means a person detained in a young offender institution or detained or imprisoned in any other institution, excluding a person on remand;

"prison governor" means a person acting as governor of a prison as required by section 7 of the Prison Act 1952;(**e**)

"provisional decision" means a decision which is not yet final because; (a) it is subject to an application for an oral hearing under rule 20(1); or (b) it is subject to reconsideration under rule 28;

"public holiday" means Christmas Day, Good Friday or a day which is a bank holiday under the Banking and Financial Dealings Act 1971(**f**) in England and Wales;

"recall" means where an offender is serving a sentence in the community on licence and the Secretary of State revokes the licence returning the offender to custody;

"request for advice" means any matter referred to the Board where it is the Board's duty to advise the Secretary of State under section 239(2) of the 2003 Act;

"solicitor" means a solicitor of the Senior Courts;

"working day" means any day which is not a Saturday, Sunday or a public holiday.

(**a**) 1952 c. 52.
(**b**) 1991 c. 53.
(**c**) Sections 227 and 228 of the 2003 Act were repealed by sections 123(c) and (d) of the Legal Aid, Sentencing and Punishment of Offenders Act 2012 c. 10, subject to savings as specified in article 5 of S.I. 2012/2906.
(**d**) 2000 c. 6. The provisions of section 85 were repealed by paragraph 1 of Schedule 37 to the 2003 Act subject to savings specified in article 3(3) of S.I. 2012/2905.
(**e**) Section 7 of the 1952 Act was amended by paragraph 1 of Schedule 5(2) to the Offender Management Act 2007 c. 21 and section 18(2) of the Sex Discrimination Act 1975 c. 65.
(**f**) 1971 c. 80.

Application

3.—(1) These Rules apply to all cases and direct applications before the Board.

(2) Subject to paragraph (3), cases referred to the Board before the date on which these Rules come into force continue under these Rules, and are treated as if the case was referred under these Rules.

(3) Applications for reconsideration under rule 28 can only be made where a decision that is eligible for reconsideration is made on or after the date these Rules come into force.

(4) Any steps taken in cases before the date on which these Rules come into force are deemed to have been taken under these Rules.

PART 2

General powers and provisions

Delegation and appointment of functions

4.—(1) The Board chair may delegate any of the Board chair's functions as set out in these Rules to any other member of the Board.

(2) The Board chair may appoint a member of the Board to carry out any function as required by the Rules.

(3) The Board chair may delegate the following functions to the Board's members of staff—

(a) the appointment of panels under rule 5;

(b) only where it is necessary to allow for a third party to comply with a deadline, and not where it would result in the adjournment or deferral of a listed hearing, the variation of—

(i) the timetable for proceedings under rule 6(3)(a), including deadlines set in directions;

(ii) the deadline for representatives to submit written representations and evidence as set in rule 18(1).

Appointment of panels

5.—(1) For all cases which have been referred to the Board, the Board chair must appoint one or more members of the Board to constitute a panel to consider, in accordance with rule 19, the release of a prisoner on the papers, or to advise the Secretary of State.

(2) If, following consideration on the papers under rule 19, a case is directed to be considered at an oral hearing, the Board chair must appoint one or more members of the Board to constitute a panel to hear that case in accordance with rules 22 to 26.

(3) If following consideration of whether a case should be decided on the papers following receipt of further evidence, in accordance with rule 21, a direction is made for the case to be decided by a panel on the papers, the Board chair must appoint one or more members of the Board to constitute a panel to make a decision on the release of the prisoner on the papers.

(4) For any application made for reconsideration of a provisional decision under rule 28, the Board chair must appoint one or more members of the Board to constitute an assessment panel to consider the application.

(5) For any application made for the Board to consider the termination of an offender's licence under rule 31, the Board chair must appoint one or more members of the Board to constitute a panel to consider the application.

(6) Any panel or assessment panel appointed under paragraphs (1) to (5) is to be chaired—

(a) where a panel or assessment panel is constituted of more than one member, by the member of the panel appointed by the Board chair for this purpose;

(b) where a panel or assessment panel is constituted of only one member, by that member.

(7) A person appointed under paragraph (1) may, in the same case, sit on a panel at an oral hearing appointed under paragraph (2).

(8) A person appointed under paragraphs (1) to (3) to consider a case on the papers or at an oral hearing must not subsequently be appointed to an assessment panel for reconsideration of that case under paragraph (4).

Case management and directions

6.—(1) A panel chair or duty member may be appointed in accordance with rule 4 to carry out case management functions and may at any time make, vary or revoke a direction.

(2) The panel chair or duty member appointed under paragraph (1) may make any direction necessary in the interests of justice, to effectively manage the case or for such other purpose as the panel chair or duty member considers appropriate.

(3) Such directions may in particular relate to—

(a) the timetable for the proceedings;

(b) the service of information or a report;

(c) the submission of evidence;

(d) the attendance of a witness or observer.

(4) A direction given under this rule may not relate to withholding information or reports; such directions are governed by rule 17.

(5) A party or third party who is subject to a direction may apply in writing for a direction to be given, varied or revoked.

(6) An application under paragraph (5) must—

(a) specify any direction or variation sought and the reasons for the direction or variation, and

(b) be served on the other party, and any third party (if applicable).

(7) Where a third party makes an application under paragraph (5), the Board must serve the application on the parties under paragraph (6)(b).

(8) Where a party, or third party, has applied for a direction to be given, varied or revoked under paragraph (5), either party or the third party (if applicable) may—

(a) make written representations about the application;

(b) where the panel chair or duty member thinks it necessary, make oral submissions at a directions hearing held under rule 7.

(9) The power to give, vary or revoke directions may be exercised in the absence of the parties.

(10) The Board must serve on the parties, and third party (if applicable), any directions given, varied or revoked as soon as practicable.

(11) The panel chair or duty member may adjourn or defer the proceedings to obtain further information or for such other purpose as they consider appropriate.

(12) Where the panel chair who is conducting an oral hearing adjourns or defers proceedings under paragraph (11) without a further hearing date being fixed, they must give the parties at least 3 weeks' notice of the date, time and place of the resumed hearing (unless the parties agree to shorter notice).

(13) Any decision to adjourn or defer an oral hearing must be recorded in writing with reasons, and that record must be provided to the parties not more than 14 days after the date of that decision.

(14) Where a prisoner's case has previously been referred to the Board, in making any decision under this rule to adjourn or defer proceedings, the panel chair or duty member must take into account the date of the decision of that prisoner's previous review.

Directions hearings

7.—(1) A panel chair or duty member may hold a directions hearing.

(2) A panel chair or duty member may direct that a third party attends a directions hearing for any purpose as the panel chair or duty member considers appropriate.

(3) The panel chair or duty member must notify the parties at least 14 days before the day of the directions hearing of the date, time, place and method fixed for the directions hearing.

(4) In specifying the method fixed for the directions hearing, the panel chair or duty member may direct that the directions hearing is to take place at a specified location or via video link, telephone conference or other electronic means.

(5) At a directions hearing, unless the panel chair or duty member directs otherwise, the panel chair or duty member must sit alone.

(6) A directions hearing may proceed in the absence of a prisoner who is represented at the hearing, or an unrepresented prisoner who chooses not to attend.

Time

8. Where the time prescribed by or under these Rules for doing any act expires on a Saturday, Sunday or public holiday, the act is deemed to be in time if it is done on the next working day.

Time limits

9. A panel chair or duty member may alter any of the time limits prescribed by or under these Rules where it is necessary to do so for the effective management of the case, in the interests of justice or for such other purpose as the panel chair or duty member considers appropriate.

Representatives

10.—(1) Subject to paragraph (2), a party may appoint a representative (whether a solicitor or barrister or other representative) to represent that party in the proceedings.

(2) The following may not act as a representative—

(a) any person who is detained or is liable to be detained under the Mental Health Act 1983(**a**);

(b) any person serving a sentence of imprisonment or a sentence of a detention;

(c) any person who is on licence having been released from a sentence of imprisonment or a sentence of detention, or

(d) any person with a conviction for an offence which remains unspent under the Rehabilitation of Offenders Act 1974(**b**).

(3) If a party appoints a representative, that party or the representative must notify the Board and the other party of the name, address and occupation of the representative at the same time as the case is referred to the Board, or as soon as reasonably practicable.

(4) Where the Secretary of State receives due notification of the appointment of a representative under paragraph (3), the Secretary of State—

(a) must provide both the prisoner and the representative with any document which is required to be provided, and

(b) may assume that the representative is and remains authorised as such until they receive written notification that this is not so from the representative or prisoner.

(5) Subject to paragraph (2), a person whose name, address and occupation has not been notified under paragraph (3) may act as a representative if authorised by the panel chair.

(**a**) 1983 c. 20.
(**b**) 1974 c. 53.

(6) If the prisoner has not appointed a representative, the panel chair or duty member may appoint a representative (solicitor or barrister or other representative) for the prisoner—

(a) with the prisoner's agreement, or

(b) where the prisoner lacks the capacity to appoint a representative and the panel chair or duty member believes that it is in the prisoner's best interests for the prisoner to be represented.

Method of service

11.—(1) Where a party or other person is required to serve documents on the Board or parties under these Rules, the documents must be served by being—

(a) sent to a secure electronic address where one has been provided by the Board and/or a party;

(b) deposited to a digital repository specified by the Board, or

(c) sent to the office of the Board and/or the party's last known address by secure post or courier.

(2) Where the Secretary of State is required to serve documents on a prisoner who is not represented, the documents must be served by handing them to the prisoner in person.

(3) The custodian who serves documents under paragraph (2) on a prisoner who is not represented must—

(a) endorse the documents with the time and date of service on the prisoner, and

(b) record that the prisoner has been served with the documents.

(4) Where a prisoner who is not represented refuses to receive documents under paragraph (3), the custodian must record the time and date that service was attempted.

(5) Any documents required to be provided to the Board and served on the Secretary of State by a prisoner who is not represented may also be served by handing the documents to a custodian addressed to the person to be served.

(6) Where a prisoner serves any documents under paragraph (5), the custodian must—

(a) endorse the documents with the time and date of receipt;

(b) record the receipt of the documents, and

(c) forward them promptly to the addressee.

Date of service

12.—(1) Unless the panel chair or duty member direct otherwise, any documents served under rule 11(1)(a) or (b) are deemed served on the next working day after the documents were transmitted.

(2) Any documents served under rule 11(1)(c) are deemed served on the second working day after the day on which the documents were posted or despatched.

(3) Any documents served under rule 11(2) or (5) are deemed served on the day the documents were handed over.

(4) Where a prisoner who is not represented refuses to receive documents under rule 11(3), the documents will be deemed as served on the day service was attempted.

Witnesses

13.—(1) A party who wishes to call a witness at an oral hearing must make a written application to the Board but such an application may not be made later than 12 weeks before the date for the oral hearing notified to the parties under rule 22.

(2) A written application to call a witness must—

(a) include the witness's name, address and occupation, and

(b) explain why the party wishes to call the witness.

(3) A party who makes an application to call a witness under paragraph (1) must, at the same time, also serve a copy of the application on the other party.

(4) A panel chair or duty member must determine an application to call a witness and must communicate this decision to the parties.

(5) The panel chair or duty member who determines the application under paragraph (4) must give reasons in writing for any refusal to call a witness.

(6) Where a panel chair or duty member makes a direction for a witness to be called, the Board must notify the parties in writing within 14 days.

(7) Written notification from the Board that it intends to call a witness must—

(a) include the witness's name, address and occupation, and

(b) explain why the witness is being called.

(8) Where a witness is called under these Rules, it is the duty of—

(a) the party calling the witness in respect of a witness called by virtue of an application under paragraph (1), and

(b) the Board, in respect of a witness called under paragraph (6),

to notify the witness no later than 2 weeks before the date of the allocated oral hearing of the date, time, place of the hearing and the need to attend.

(9) Where a panel chair or duty member has directed that a witness is to be called, the panel chair or duty member may direct that it is suitable for a witness to attend via video link, telephone conference or other electronic means.

Observers

14.—(1) A party who wishes to be accompanied at an oral hearing by an observer must make a written application to the Board but such an application may not be made later than 12 weeks before the date allocated for the oral hearing under rule 22.

(2) A party who makes an application to be accompanied by an observer under paragraph (1) must, at the same time, also serve a copy of the application on the other party.

(3) Within 14 days of the receipt of the application under paragraph (2), the other party may make representations to the Board on the application.

(4) After the 14-day period for the other party to make representations under paragraph (3) has expired, the panel chair or duty member must determine the application for a party to be accompanied by an observer and communicate this decision to the parties.

(5) Before granting an application made under paragraph (1), the panel chair or duty member must obtain the agreement of—

(a) the prison governor or prison director, where the hearing is being held in a prison, or

(b) in any other circumstance, the person who appears to the panel chair or duty member to have the authority to agree to the admittance of the proposed observer to the premises.

Location and privacy of oral hearings

15.—(1) An oral hearing must be held via video link, telephone conference or other electronic means if the duty member or panel chair so directs.

(2) In any other circumstance, the oral hearing must be held at such a place as the duty member or panel chair, with the agreement of the Secretary of State, directs.

(3) An oral hearing (including a directions hearing) must be held in private.

(4) In addition to any witness who has been called under these Rules, and any observer whose attendance has been approved under rule 14, the panel chair or duty member may—

(a) admit any other person to the oral hearing as an observer, and

(b) impose conditions on that person's admittance.

(5) At the oral hearing, the parties may not challenge the attendance of any witness who has been called under these Rules, or observer whose attendance has been approved under rule 14 or under paragraph (4).

PART 3

Parole Board proceedings

Referral and service of reports

16.—(1) A case is deemed to be referred to the Board on the date that the Board receives the referral letter and the information and reports required under paragraph (3) from the Secretary of State.

(2) The Secretary of State must serve the information and reports required under paragraph (3) on the prisoner (and the prisoner's representative if they are represented) at the same time as service on the Board.

(3) Subject to rule 17, the Secretary of State must serve on the Board and the prisoner (and the prisoner's representative if they are represented)—

(a) the information specified in the Schedule;

(b) any further information which the Secretary of State considers relevant to the case, and

(c) where a case relates to a request for advice, any information which the Secretary of State considers relevant to the case.

Withholding information or reports

17.—(1) The Secretary of State and any third party authorised by the Secretary of State ("authorised third party") may apply to the Board for information or any report ("the material") to be withheld from the prisoner, or from both the prisoner and their representative, where the Secretary of State or the authorised third party considers—

(a) that its disclosure would adversely affect—

(i) national security;

(ii) the prevention of disorder or crime, or

(iii) the health or welfare of the prisoner or any other person, and

(b) that withholding the material is a necessary and proportionate measure in the circumstances of the case.

(2) An application under paragraph (1) may not be made later than 8 weeks before the date allocated for an oral hearing under rule 22.

(3) Where the Secretary of State or the authorised third party makes an application for the material to be withheld under paragraph (1), the Secretary of State or authorised third party must serve on the Board—

(a) the material, or a separate document containing the material, and

(b) a written application for non-disclosure, explaining why it is proposed to be withheld.

(4) On receipt of an application under paragraph (3)(b), either a panel chair or duty member appointed for that purpose, must consider the application and may make directions as necessary to enable determination of the application.

(5) Where the panel chair or duty member is satisfied that all relevant information has been served on the Board, they must consider the application and direct that the material should be—

(a) served on the prisoner and their representative (if applicable) in full;

(b) withheld from the prisoner or from both the prisoner and their representative, or

(c) disclosed to the prisoner, or to both the prisoner and the prisoner's representative (if applicable) in the form of a summary or redacted version.

(6) If—

(a) a direction is given under paragraph (5)(a) and the Secretary of State or authorised third party intends to appeal against it in accordance with paragraph (11), or

(b) a direction is given under paragraph (5)(b) or (c),

the Secretary of State, or the Board (where an authorised third party made the application under paragraph (3)), must, as soon as practicable, notify the prisoner and the prisoner's representative (if applicable) that an application has been made under paragraph (3)(b) and the direction that has been made under paragraph (5).

(7) If the panel chair or duty member appointed under paragraph (4) gives a direction under paragraph (5)(b) or (c) that relates only to the prisoner, and that prisoner has a representative, the Secretary of State or authorised third party must, subject to paragraphs (10) and (11), serve the material as soon as practicable (unless the panel chair or duty member directs otherwise) on the prisoner's representative, if the representative is—

(a) a barrister or solicitor;

(b) a registered medical practitioner, or

(c) a person whom the panel chair or duty member appointed under paragraph (4) directs is suitable by virtue of their experience or professional qualifications.

(8) The panel chair or duty member may direct the appointment of a special advocate appointed by the Attorney General to represent the prisoner's interests where the panel chair or duty member appointed under paragraph (4)—

(a) makes a direction under (5)(a) and the Secretary of State or the authorised third party appeals the direction under paragraph (11), or

(b) makes a direction under (5)(b) or (c) that relates to a prisoner and their representative, or the prisoner does not have a representative.

(9) If a direction to appoint a special advocate is made under paragraph (8), the Secretary of State or authorised third party must serve the material as soon as practicable (unless the panel chair or duty member directs otherwise) on the special advocate.

(10) The material must not be disclosed to the prisoner's representative under paragraph (7) unless the prisoner's representative first gives an undertaking to the Board that the prisoner's representative will not, without the consent of the panel chair or duty member, disclose it to the prisoner or to any other person.

(11) Within 7 days of notification by the Secretary of State or Board in accordance with paragraph (6), either party or the authorised third party may appeal against that direction to the Board chair and notify the other party of the application to appeal.

(12) If the Secretary of State or authorised third party appeals the direction in accordance with paragraph (11), the Secretary of State or authorised third party need not serve the material under paragraphs (5) or (7) until the appeal is determined.

(13) Where a direction is made under paragraph (5)(b) or (c) to withhold material from a prisoner who does not have a representative, the decision will automatically be considered in an appeal to the Board chair.

(14) Within 7 days of being notified that a party has appealed under paragraph (11), the other party may make representations in respect of the appeal to the Board chair.

(15) If—

(a) a panel chair or duty member appointed under paragraph (4) to determine an application under paragraph (1), or

(b) the Board chair determining an appeal under paragraph (11) or (13),

decides that any material which is subject to the application by the Secretary of State or authorised third party under paragraph (1) should be disclosed to the prisoner (in full or in the form of a summary or redacted version), the Secretary of State or authorised third party may withdraw the material within 7 days of that decision.

(16) If the Secretary of State or authorised third party withdraws any material in accordance with paragraph (15), no one who has seen that material may be a member of a panel which determines the case.

Representations by and evidence of the parties

18.—(1) A party who wishes to make representations to the Board must serve them on the Board and the other party—

(a) within 4 weeks of the case being referred to the Board where the case relates to the initial release of a prisoner, or

(b) at the time of referral if the case relates to the release following recall of a prisoner.

(2) Any additional evidence that a party wishes to present at an oral hearing must be served on the Board and the other party at least 14 days before the date of the oral hearing.

(3) Any party that wishes to present at an oral hearing documentary evidence which has not been served at least 14 days before the date of the hearing, must serve the material on the Board and the other party, together with an application to the panel chair or duty member for permission to do so, as soon as reasonably practicable, and must, as part of that application, give reasons for late service.

Consideration on the papers

19.—(1) Where a panel is appointed under rule 5(1) to consider the release of a prisoner, the panel must decide on the papers either that—

(a) the prisoner is suitable for release;

(b) the prisoner is unsuitable for release, or

(c) the case should be directed to an oral hearing.

(2) Where a panel has received a request for advice from the Secretary of State concerning whether a prisoner should move to open conditions, the panel must recommend whether—

(a) the prisoner is suitable for a move to open conditions, or

(b) the prisoner is not suitable for a move to open conditions.

(3) Where a panel makes a decision that the case should be directed to an oral hearing under this rule, the panel may at the same time make any directions relating to the oral hearing.

(4) Any decision made under paragraph (1)(a) which is eligible for reconsideration under rule 28 is provisional, and becomes final if no application for reconsideration is received within the period specified by that rule.

(5) Any decision made under paragraph (1)(a) which is not eligible for reconsideration under rule 28 is final.

(6) Any decision made under paragraph (1)(b) is provisional.

(7) Where the Board receives a request for advice with respect to any matter referred to it by the Secretary of State, the Board may advise or make a recommendation to the Secretary of State without an oral hearing.

(8) The decision or advice of the panel must be recorded in writing with reasons for that decision or advice, and the written record provided to the parties within 14 days of that decision or advice.

Procedure after a provisional decision on the papers

20.—(1) Where a panel appointed under rule 5(1) has made a decision that a prisoner is unsuitable for release under rule 19(1)(b), the prisoner may apply in writing for a panel at an oral hearing to determine the case.

(2) A prisoner who makes an application under paragraph (1) must serve the application, together with reasons for making an application, on the Board and the Secretary of State, within 28 days of the provision of the written record under rule 19(8).

(3) If no application has been served by the prisoner under paragraph (2) after the expiry of the period specified by that paragraph, a provisional decision made under rule 19(1)(b)—

(a) remains provisional if it is eligible for reconsideration under rule 28, and becomes final if no application for reconsideration is received within the period specified by that rule, or

(b) becomes final if it is not eligible for reconsideration under rule 28.

(4) Where no application is served by a prisoner under paragraph (2), the decision must be provided to the parties by the Board within 35 days of the written record under rule 19(8).

(5) If an application is served in accordance with paragraph (2), the decision about whether the case should be determined at an oral hearing must be taken by a member of the Board who—

(a) is a duty member, and

(b) was not part of the constituted panel appointed under rule 5(1) who made the provisional decision.

(6) If the decision taken under paragraph (5) is that the case should not be determined at an oral hearing, a provisional decision under rule 19(1)(b)—

(a) remains provisional if it is eligible for reconsideration under rule 28 and becomes final if no application for reconsideration is received within the period specified by that rule, or

(b) becomes final if it is not eligible for reconsideration under rule 28.

(7) Where the decision taken under paragraph (5) is that the case should not be determined at an oral hearing, that decision must be provided to the parties by the Board within 35 days of the written record under rule 19(8).

(8) A decision under paragraph (5) cannot be deferred or adjourned by a panel chair or duty member under rule 6 and the time limit in paragraph (7) cannot be extended under rule 9.

Decision on the papers after a direction for an oral hearing

21.—(1) Subject to the provisions of this rule, where further evidence is received by the Board after a panel have directed that a case should be determined at an oral hearing under rule 19(1)(c) or 20(5), a panel chair or duty member can direct that the case should be decided on the papers if an oral hearing is no longer necessary.

(2) Where further evidence is received under paragraph (1), the Board must notify the parties of the receipt of the evidence as soon as practicable.

(3) Within 14 days of notification of the receipt of further evidence under paragraph (2), the parties may make representations on—

(a) the contents of the further evidence, and

(b) whether they agree to the case being decided by a panel on the papers.

(4) After the 14-day period for the parties to make representations under paragraph (3), the panel chair or duty member will consider the further evidence and any representations made, and make a direction that the case should—

(a) be decided by a panel on the papers, or

(b) continue to be determined by a panel at an oral hearing under rule 25.

(5) Where a direction is made under paragraph (4)(a) for a decision to be made by a panel on the papers under paragraph (7), the panel may be constituted of the panel chair who made the direction or by a new panel appointed under rule 5(3).

(6) A direction for a case to be decided on the papers under paragraph (4)(a) cannot be made where there is less than 3 weeks until the oral hearing.

(7) Where a direction is made that the case should be decided on the papers under paragraph (4)(a), the panel must decide either that—

(a) the prisoner is suitable for release, or

(b) the prisoner is not suitable for release.

(8) Any decision made under paragraph (7) is provisional if it is eligible for reconsideration under rule 28, and becomes final if no application for reconsideration is received within the period specified by that rule.

(9) Any decision made under paragraph (7) which is not eligible for reconsideration under rule 28 is final.

(10) Where a panel chair or duty member receives a request for advice from the Secretary of State concerning whether a prisoner should move to open conditions, the panel chair must recommend whether—

(a) the prisoner is suitable for a move to open conditions, or

(b) the prisoner is not suitable for a move to open conditions.

(11) Where the Board receive a request for advice with respect to any matter referred to it by the Secretary of State, any recommendation made in respect of that request is final.

(12) The decision under paragraph (7) and/or recommendation under paragraph (10) must be recorded in writing with reasons for that decision and/or recommendation, and the written record provided to the parties within 14 days of that decision and/or recommendation.

Notice of an oral hearing

22.—(1) Before fixing the date of the oral hearing the Board must consult the parties.

(2) Within 1 week of a case being listed, the Board must notify the parties of the date of the oral hearing.

(3) The Board must give the parties reasonable notice of the date, time and place of the hearing.

(4) Where notification is less than 12 weeks then the Board must review any other affected timescale.

(5) Notification of less than 3 weeks must be agreed with both parties.

(6) If applicable, the Board must give the parties notice that the hearing will be held via video link, telephone conference or other electronic means.

Notification by prisoner

23.—(1) A prisoner must notify the Board and the Secretary of State if—

(a) the prisoner does not want a panel at an oral hearing to consider the case, or

(b) the prisoner does not want to attend an oral hearing which has been listed.

(2) An oral hearing may take place in the absence of a prisoner where—

(a) a prisoner has notified the Board in accordance with paragraph (1);

(b) a represented prisoner has not notified the Board in accordance with paragraph (1) but the prisoner's representative is in attendance;

(c) a represented prisoner has not notified the Board in accordance with paragraph (1) and neither the prisoner nor the prisoner's representative are present at the hearing.

Oral hearing procedure

24.—(1) At the beginning of the oral hearing the panel chair must—

(a) explain the order of proceedings which the panel plans to adopt, and

(b) invite each party present to state their view as to the suitability of the prisoner for release or for transfer to open conditions, as applicable.

(2) The panel—

(a) must avoid formality during the hearing;

12

(b) may ask any question to satisfy itself of the level of risk of the prisoner, and

(c) must conduct the hearing in a manner it considers most suitable to the clarification of the issues before it and to the just handling of the proceedings.

(3) The parties are entitled to—

(a) take such part in the proceedings as the panel thinks fit;

(b) hear each other's witnesses and representations;

(c) put questions to each other;

(d) call a witness who has been given written notification in accordance with rule 13, and

(e) question any witness appearing before the panel.

(4) If, in the opinion of the panel chair, any person at the hearing is behaving in a disruptive manner, the panel chair may require that person to leave.

(5) The panel chair may permit a person who was required to leave under paragraph (4) to return on such conditions as the panel chair may specify.

(6) A panel may produce or receive in evidence any document or information whether or not it would be admissible in a court of law.

(7) No person is compelled to give any evidence or produce any document which they could not be compelled to give or produce on the trial of an action.

(8) The panel chair may require any person present to leave the hearing where evidence which has been directed to be withheld from the prisoner or the prisoner and their representative under rule 17 is to be considered.

(9) After all the evidence has been given, if the prisoner is present at the hearing, the prisoner must be given an opportunity to address the panel.

Decision by a panel at an oral hearing

25.—(1) Where a panel has considered a prisoner's case at an oral hearing, the panel must decide either that—

(a) the prisoner is suitable for release, or

(b) the prisoner is unsuitable for release.

(2) Any decision made by the panel under paragraph (1) which is eligible for reconsideration under rule 28 is provisional, and becomes final if no application for reconsideration is received within the period specified by that rule.

(3) Any decision made by the panel under paragraph (1) which is not eligible for reconsideration under rule 28 is final.

(4) Where a panel receives a request for advice from the Secretary of State concerning whether a prisoner should move to open conditions, the panel must recommend either that—

(a) the prisoner is suitable for a move to open conditions, or

(b) the prisoner is not suitable for a move to open conditions.

(5) Where the Board receives a request for advice with respect to any matter referred to it by the Secretary of State, any recommendation made in respect of that request is final.

(6) The decision under paragraph (1) and/or recommendation under paragraph (4) must be recorded in writing with reasons, and that record must be provided to the parties not more than 14 days after the end of the hearing.

(7) The recorded decision and/or recommendation must refer only to the matter which the Secretary of State referred to the Board.

Decision making by a panel at an oral hearing

26.—(1) Where a panel has been appointed under rule 5(2), a decision of the majority of the members of the panel is the decision of the oral panel.

(2) A panel for an oral hearing that is unable to reach a decision in accordance with paragraph (1) must be dissolved by the Board chair, who must then appoint a new panel.

Summaries and disclosure

27.—(1) Where a victim or any other person seeks disclosure of a summary of the reasons for a decision—

(a) made under rule 19(1)(a), 21(7), 25(1) or 31(6);

(b) made under rule 19(1)(b) where a prisoner does not make an application for an oral hearing under rule 20(1), or a prisoner makes an application for an oral hearing but it is decided that the case should not be considered at an oral hearing under rule 20(6),

the Board must produce a summary of the reasons for that decision, unless the Board chair considers that there are exceptional circumstances why a summary should not be produced for disclosure.

(2) The Board is not required to produce a summary under paragraph (1) where the request is made more than 6 months after the decision.

(3) Where a victim seeks disclosure of a summary produced under paragraph (1), the Secretary of State must notify the Board that the victim wishes to receive a summary, and must disclose the summary that is produced by the Board to that victim.

(4) Where any other person seeks disclosure of a summary under paragraph (1), the Board must disclose the summary that is produced to that person.

(5) Subject to paragraph (1), information about proceedings under these Rules must not be disclosed, except insofar as the Board chair directs.

(6) Other than those of the parties, the names of persons concerned in proceedings under these Rules must not be disclosed under paragraphs (1) to (5).

(7) A contravention of paragraphs (5) or (6), is actionable as a breach of statutory duty by any person who suffers loss or damage as a result.

(8) For the purposes of this rule—

"victim" means a person who is participating in the Victim Contact Scheme in respect of a prisoner who is party to proceedings under these Rules;

"Victim Contact Scheme" means the scheme set out in the Victims' Code in accordance with section 32 of the Domestic Violence, Crime and Victims Act 2004(**a**).

Reconsideration of decisions

28.—(1) Subject to paragraph (2), where a decision has been made under rule 19(1)(a) or (b), 21(7) or 25(1), a party may apply to the Board for the case to be reconsidered on the grounds that the decision is—

(a) irrational, or

(b) procedurally unfair.

(2) Decisions are eligible for reconsideration only where the prisoner is serving—

(a) an indeterminate sentence;

(b) an extended sentence;

(c) a determinate sentence subject to initial release by the Board under Chapter 6 of Part 12 of the 2003 Act.

(**a**) 2004 c. 28. Section 33(6) requires the Code to be laid before Parliament and was amended by paragraph 10(2) of Schedule 1 to the Secretary of State for Justice Order 2007 (S.I. 2007/2128).

(3) An application for a provisional decision to be reconsidered under paragraph (1) must be made and served on the other party no later than 21 days after the written decision recorded under rules 19(8), 21(12) or 25(6) is provided to the parties.

(4) Where a party makes an application under paragraph (3), the other party may make representations, and those representations must be provided to the Board and the party who made the application within 7 days of service of the application.

(5) Where an application made under paragraph (3) is received by the Board, the application must be considered on the papers by an assessment panel.

(6) After assessing the application under paragraph (5), the assessment panel must—

(a) direct that the provisional decision should be reconsidered, or

(b) dismiss the application.

(7) The assessment panel may direct that the provisional decision should be reconsidered under paragraph (6)(a) only if it has identified a ground for reconsideration under paragraph (1).

(8) Where the assessment panel dismiss the application under paragraph (6)(b), the provisional decision becomes final.

(9) Where the assessment panel directs that the provisional decision should be reconsidered under paragraph (6)(a), the assessment panel must direct that the case should be—

(a) reconsidered on the papers by the previous panel or a new panel appointed under rule 5(1), or

(b) reconsidered at an oral hearing by the previous panel or a new panel appointed under rule 5(2).

(10) The decision of the assessment panel must be recorded in writing with reasons, and that record must be provided to the parties not more than 14 days after the decision.

Error of Procedure

29. Where there has been an error of procedure by either party or by the Board, including a failure to comply with a rule—

(a) the error does not invalidate any step taken in the proceedings unless the member appointed by the Board for this purpose, being either a panel chair or duty member, directs otherwise, either on the application of a party or in the course of conducting the proceedings, and

(b) the panel chair or duty member may make a direction or take any other step that it considers appropriate.

Slip Rule

30.—(1) The Board may at any time correct an accidental slip or omission in a decision.

(2) A party may apply for a correction without notice.

PART 4

Termination of licence

Applications to terminate IPP licences

31.—(1) Where an offender qualifies to make an application to terminate their licence under section 31A of the 1997 Act(**a**), the offender may make a direct application to the Board or apply through the Secretary of State.

(**a**) Section 31A of the 1997 Act was inserted by the 2003 Act and has been amended by section 117(10)(a) of the Legal Aid, Sentencing and Punishment of Offenders Act 2012 c. 10, and paragraph 141 of Schedule 16 to the Armed Forces Act 2006 c. 52.

(2) Where an offender makes a direct application, the Board must serve the application on the Secretary of State and the Secretary of State must serve any reports or evidence as directed by the Board.

(3) Where an application is made through the Secretary of State, the Secretary of State must serve any reports or evidence at the same time as sending the application to the Board.

(4) Where the Board receives an application, either from the offender directly or through the Secretary of State, a panel appointed under rule 5(5) must consider the application in accordance with section 31A(4) of the 1997 Act.

(5) In considering the application under paragraphs (2) or (3), the panel may—

(a) make a decision on the papers, or

(b) direct that the application should be decided by a panel at a hearing.

(6) Where a panel considers the application on the papers or at a hearing, it must decide to—

(a) terminate the offender's licence;

(b) amend the offender's licence in accordance with section 31(3) of the 1997 Act, or

(c) refuse the application.

(7) Where a decision is made by a panel under paragraph (6), the Board must record that decision in writing with reasons for that decision, and that record must be provided to the offender and Secretary of State within 14 days of the decision.

Robert Buckland
20th June 2019 Ministry of Justice

SCHEDULE

Rule 16

Information and reports for a reference to the Board by the Secretary of State to determine the initial release of a prisoner or to determine the re-release of a recalled prisoner

Part A

Information relating to the prisoner

1. The full name of the prisoner.

2. The date of birth of the prisoner.

3. The prison in which the prisoner is detained, details of any other prisons in which the pisoner has been detained under the current sentence, and the date of and the reason for any transfer.

4. The date on which the prisoner was given the current sentence, details of the offence and any previous convictions.

5. If available, the comments of the trial judge when passing sentence.

6. The parole history, if any, of the prisoner, including details of any periods spent on licence during the current sentence.

7. If available, the conclusions of the Court of Appeal in respect of any appeal by the prisoner against conviction or sentence.

8. In recall cases, the details of any previous recalls of the prisoner, including the reasons for such recalls and subsequent re-release on licence.

9. In recall cases, the statement of reasons for the most recent recall, including the outcome of any criminal charges laid against the prisoner prior, or subsequent, to the point at which the prisoner was recalled.

10. In recall cases, if available, witness statements, police statements and the CPS summary of any alleged offending on licence.

Part B

Reports relating to the prisoner

1. If available and relevant to the Secretary of State's assessment of risk, the pre-trial and pre-sentence reports examined by the sentencing court on the circumstances of the offence, including any specialist reports produced at sentencing.

2. If available, any reports or evidence the sentencing court recommended be seen by those considering future risk.

3. Reports on a prisoner who was subject to a transfer direction under section 47 of the Mental Health Act 1983.

4. Current reports on prisoner's risk factors, reduction in risk and performance and behaviour in prison, including views on suitability for release on licence as well as compliance with any sentence plan.

5. A current risk management report prepared for the Board by an officer of the National Probation Service or relevant Community Rehabilitation Company, including information on the following where relevant —

(a) details of the prisoner's address, family circumstances and family attitudes towards the prisoner;

(b) alternative options if the offender cannot return home;

(c) the opportunity for employment on release;

(d) the local community's attitude towards the prisoner (if known);

(e) the prisoner's attitude towards the offence for which the offender received the sentence that is being considered by the Parole Board;

(f) the prisoners' response to previous periods of supervision;

(g) the prisoner's behaviour during any temporary leave during the current sentence;

(h) the prisoner's attitude to the prospect of release and the requirements and objectives of supervision, including likely compliance;

(i) an assessment of the risk of reoffending;

(j) a programme of supervision;

(k) analysis of the impact of the offence on the victims, for which the offender received the sentence which is being considered by the Board;

(l) a view on the suitability for release;

(m) recommendations regarding any licence conditions.

6. If available, a current Victim Personal Statement setting out the impact the offence has had on the victim and/or the victim's family.

7. In recall cases, any reports considered by the Secretary of state in deciding to recall the prisoner.

8. In recall cases, a copy of the prisoner's licence at the point at which the Secretary of State decided to recall the prisoner.

EXPLANATORY NOTE

(This note is not part of the Rules)

These Rules set out the procedure to be adopted by the Parole Board ("the Board") when dealing with cases referred to it by the Secretary of State and when receiving direct applications from prisoners in relation to reconsideration and termination of Imprisonment for Public Protection (IPP) and Detention for Public Protection (DPP) licences.

Part 1 revokes the Parole Board Rules 2016 (S.I. 2016/1041) and the Parole Board (Amendment) Rules 2018 (S.I. 2018/541), and contains provisions for the application and interpretation of the Rules.

Part 2 covers the powers of the Board and provisions that apply generally across the whole parole process, including the appointment of panels, the power of members to make directions, the appointment of representatives, and the power to call witnesses and allow the admittance of observers.

Rule 4 gives the Board chair the power to delegate any of the Board chair's functions in the Rules to any other member of the Board. The Board chair may also appoint any member of the Board to carry out any function. Members of staff can be empowered by the Board chair to appoint panels and make variations to directions where it is necessary to allow a third party to comply with a deadline only where it would not result in the adjournment or deferral of a listed hearing.

Rule 5 provides for the appointment of panels for paper hearings, oral hearings, the consideration of whether to return a case to a paper hearing following the receipt of further evidence, the consideration of applications for reconsideration and the consideration of applications for the termination of an offender's licence. The rule also sets out the members that are to chair the various panels.

Rule 6 sets out the powers of members of the Board to make, vary and revoke directions in order to manage the cases before the Board.

Rule 7 sets out the procedure to be followed for a directions hearing.

Rule 8 provides for acts to be deemed to be completed if a time limit prescribed by the Rules expires on a Saturday, Sunday or public holiday.

Rule 9 gives a panel chair or duty member the power to amend any of the time limits set out in, or made under, the Rules.

Rule 10 sets out the procedure to be followed by the parties when appointing a representative. The rule also gives the panel chair or duty member the power to appoint a representative for the prisoner with the prisoner's agreement, or where the prisoner does not have the capacity to appoint a representative on their own behalf and it is in the prisoner's best interests to be represented.

Rule 11 prescribes the methods of service available to the parties.

Rule 12 provides for when service will be deemed to have taken place when carried out as dictated by rule 11.

Rule 13 sets out the procedure for parties making applications to the Board for witnesses to be called at an oral hearing. Rule 13(9) allows the panel chair or duty member to direct that a witness may attend remotely i.e. by electronic means.

Rule 14 sets out the procedure for parties to apply for observers to attend oral hearings.

Rule 15 sets out the methods by which an oral hearing can take place – in person, by video link, telephone conference or other electronic means. The rule governs that oral hearings, including directions hearings, must be held in private. Only the parties and witnesses and observers who have been allowed to attend under the Rules may be present at an oral hearing. The panel chair or duty member may allow for the attendance of an observer on the day of the hearing itself.

Part 3 sets out the procedure to be followed for the entire Parole Board process from the referral of the case and service of information, through consideration by a panel on the papers, to oral hearings.

Rule 16 provides that, on the date the Board receive the referral letter and the necessary information and reports under the Schedule from the Secretary of State, the case is deemed to have been referred. The necessary information and reports must also be served on the prisoner and the prisoner's representative on the same day as service on the Board. Rule 16(3) sets out the information that must be served at the same time as referral.

Rule 17 sets out the procedure for withholding information from the prisoner or both the prisoner and the prisoner's representative where its disclosure would have an adverse effect on national security, the prevention of disorder or crime, or the health or welfare of the prisoner or any other person. Only the Secretary of State and authorised third parties may apply to the Board for material to be withheld from the prisoner or the prisoner and their representative under this Rule. This rule provides that where a direction is made for the material to be withheld from an unrepresented prisoner, that decision will automatically be considered in an appeal without the necessity of the prisoner having to apply for an appeal.

Rule 18 provides the procedure for the parties making representations to the Board and for serving any additional evidence for an oral hearing.

Rule 19 gives the panel the power to make a decision on the papers in respect of the release of offenders (including prisoners serving indeterminate sentences). Under this rule, the Board can also direct that a case should be considered at an oral hearing. A decision that a prisoner is suitable for release under rule19(1)(a) is provisional if it is eligible for reconsideration under rule 28. If the decision is not eligible for reconsideration it is final. A decision that a prisoner is not suitable for release under rule 19(1)(b) is provisional to allow the prisoner to apply for the case to be determined at an oral hearing under rule 20.

Rule 20 allows, and sets out the procedure, for a prisoner who has been found on the papers to be unsuitable for release to apply for the case to be determined at an oral hearing. This rule provides that where a prisoner does not apply for the case to be determined at an oral hearing or an application is made but the panel chair or duty member decide that the case should not be determined at an oral hearing, the decision made under rule 19 remains provisional if it is eligible for reconsideration under rule 28, otherwise it is final.

Rule 21 provides that, where the panel have made a direction for a case to be considered at an oral hearing, a panel chair or duty member can direct that the case should be decided by a panel on the papers if further information has been supplied to the Board which makes an oral hearing unnecessary. A case cannot be directed back to be decided on the papers where there is less than three weeks until the date listed for oral hearing. Where a direction is made for a case to be decided on the papers under this rule, the decision that is made by the panel chair or by the panel appointed under rule 5(3) remains provisional if it is eligible for reconsideration. If it is not eligible for reconsideration, it is final.

Rules 22 to 24 set out the procedure for a case to be considered at an oral hearing.

Rule 25 provides for the panel to make a decision on release following an oral hearing. A decision made under rule 25 remains provisional if it is eligible for reconsideration, otherwise it is final.

Rule 26 sets out that a decision of an oral panel is the decision of the majority of the panel. Any panel that is unable to reach a decision must be dissolved by the Board chair and a new panel appointed.

Rule 27 provides that the Board must produce a summary of the reasons for certain decisions made under rules 19, 21, 25 and 31, for a victim or any other person who makes an application to receive one, unless there are exceptional circumstances for why a summary should not be produced for disclosure. Where a decision is made under rule 19(1)(b) that a prisoner is not suitable for release, a victim or other person will be able to apply for a summary of the reasons for that decision only if the case is not directed to be considered at an oral hearing (either because the prisoner did not apply for it to be considered at an oral hearing or the application was refused).

Any information about proceedings before the Board must not be disclosed except as directed by the Board chair. The names of other persons concerned in Board proceedings must never be disclosed. A contravention of the rules against disclosure are actionable as a breach of statutory duty.

Rule 28 sets out the power for the Board to consider applications from a party for a case to be reconsidered where a decision has been made by a panel on the papers or following an oral hearing. The power to reconsider a case applies to indeterminate sentences, all extended sentences and determinate sentences where initial release is not automatic and is instead decided by the Board. A party may apply for a case to be reconsidered on the grounds that the decision was irrational or procedurally unfair. An assessment panel will consider an application and decide whether that case meets the grounds for reconsideration or whether the application should be dismissed. If the panel directs that the case should be reconsidered, the panel must direct the case back to a panel to decide the case again on the papers or at an oral hearing.

Rule 29 provides for the procedure where an error of procedure is made by a party or the Board.

Rule 30 allows for the correction of any slip or omission in a decision.

Part 4 governs the procedure for considering applications made by offenders serving Imprisonment or Detention for Public Protection ("IPP/DPP") sentences for their licence to be terminated under section 31A of the Crime (Sentences) Act 1997 ("the 1997 Act"). Section 31A of the 1997 Act allows for offenders serving IPP or DPP sentences who have been released on licence to apply to the Board for their licence to be terminated if a period of ten years has passed, beginning with the date of release. Section 31A of the 1997 Act sets out that the Board shall direct that the Secretary of State make an order that the licence is to cease to have effect if it is satisfied that it is no longer necessary for the protection of the public that the licence should remain in force. If the Board is not satisfied of this, it must dismiss the application,

A full impact assessment of the effect that this instrument will have on the costs of business, the voluntary sector and the public sector is available from www.legislation.gov.uk.

Printed and published in the UK by The Stationery Office Limited under the authority and superintendence of Jeff James, Controller of Her Majesty's Stationery Office and Queen's Printer of Acts of Parliament.

MORE BOOKS BY LAW BRIEF PUBLISHING

A selection of our other titles available now:-

'A Practical Guide to the Independent School Standards – September 2023 Edition' by Sarah McKimm
'A Practical Guide to Estate Administration and Crypto Assets' by Richard Marshall
'A Practical Guide to Managing GDPR Data Subject Access Requests – Second Edition' by Patrick O'Kane
'A Practical Guide to Parental Alienation in Private and Public Law Children Cases' by Sam King QC & Frankie Shama
'Contested Heritage – Removing Art from Land and Historic Buildings' by Richard Harwood QC, Catherine Dobson, David Sawtell
'The Limits of Separate Legal Personality: When Those Running a Company Can Be Held Personally Liable for Losses Caused to Third Parties Outside of the Company' by Dr Mike Wilkinson
'A Practical Guide to Transgender Law' by Robin Moira White & Nicola Newbegin
'A Practical Guide to 'Stranded Spouses' in Family Law' by Mani Singh Basi
'A Practical Guide to Residential Freehold Conveyancing' by Lorraine Richardson
'A Practical Guide to Pensions on Divorce for Lawyers' by Bryan Scant
'A Practical Guide to Challenging Sham Marriage Allegations in Immigration Law' by Priya Solanki
'A Practical Guide to Digital Communications Evidence in Criminal Law' by Sam Willis
'A Practical Guide to Legal Rights in Scotland' by Sarah-Jane Macdonald
'A Practical Guide to New Build Conveyancing' by Paul Sams & Rebecca East
'A Practical Guide to Defending Barristers in Disciplinary Cases' by Marc Beaumont
'A Practical Guide to Inherited Wealth on Divorce' by Hayley Trim
'A Practical Guide to Practice Direction 12J and Domestic Abuse in Private Law Children Proceedings' by Rebecca Cross & Malvika Jaganmohan

'A Practical Guide to Confiscation and Restraint' by Narita Bahra QC, John Carl Townsend, David Winch
'A Practical Guide to the Law of Forests in Scotland' by Philip Buchan
'A Practical Guide to Health and Medical Cases in Immigration Law' by Rebecca Chapman & Miranda Butler
'A Practical Guide to Bad Character Evidence for Criminal Practitioners by Aparna Rao
'A Practical Guide to Extradition Law post-Brexit' by Myles Grandison et al
'A Practical Guide to Hoarding and Mental Health for Housing Lawyers' by Rachel Coyle
'A Practical Guide to Psychiatric Claims in Personal Injury – 2nd Edition' by Liam Ryan
'Stephens on Contractual Indemnities' by Richard Stephens
'A Practical Guide to the EU Succession Regulation' by Richard Frimston
'A Practical Guide to Solicitor and Client Costs – 2nd Edition' by Robin Dunne
'Constructive Dismissal – Practice Pointers and Principles' by Benjimin Burgher
'A Practical Guide to Religion and Belief Discrimination Claims in the Workplace' by Kashif Ali
'A Practical Guide to the Law of Medical Treatment Decisions' by Ben Troke
'Fundamental Dishonesty and QOCS in Personal Injury Proceedings: Law and Practice' by Jake Rowley
'A Practical Guide to the Law in Relation to School Exclusions' by Charlotte Hadfield & Alice de Coverley
'A Practical Guide to Divorce for the Silver Separators' by Karin Walker
'The Right to be Forgotten – The Law and Practical Issues' by Melissa Stock
'A Practical Guide to Planning Law and Rights of Way in National Parks, the Broads and AONBs' by James Maurici QC, James Neill et al
'A Practical Guide to Election Law' by Tom Tabori
'A Practical Guide to the Law in Relation to Surrogacy' by Andrew Powell
'A Practical Guide to Claims Arising from Fatal Accidents – 2nd Edition' by James Patience
'A Practical Guide to the Ownership of Employee Inventions – From Entitlement to Compensation' by James Tumbridge & Ashley Roughton
'A Practical Guide to Asbestos Claims' by Jonathan Owen & Gareth McAloon

'A Practical Guide to Stamp Duty Land Tax in England and Northern Ireland' by Suzanne O'Hara
'A Practical Guide to the Law of Farming Partnerships' by Philip Whitcomb
'Covid-19, Homeworking and the Law – The Essential Guide to Employment and GDPR Issues' by Forbes Solicitors
'Covid-19 and Criminal Law – The Essential Guide' by Ramya Nagesh
'Covid-19 and Family Law in England and Wales – The Essential Guide' by Safda Mahmood
'A Practical Guide to the Law of Unlawful Eviction and Harassment – 2nd Edition' by Stephanie Lovegrove
'Covid-19, Brexit and the Law of Commercial Leases – The Essential Guide' by Mark Shelton
'A Practical Guide to Costs in Personal Injury Claims – 2nd Edition' by Matthew Hoe
'A Practical Guide to the General Data Protection Regulation (GDPR) – 2nd Edition' by Keith Markham
'Ellis on Credit Hire – Sixth Edition' by Aidan Ellis & Tim Kevan
'A Practical Guide to Working with Litigants in Person and McKenzie Friends in Family Cases' by Stuart Barlow
'Protecting Unregistered Brands: A Practical Guide to the Law of Passing Off' by Lorna Brazell
'A Practical Guide to Secondary Liability and Joint Enterprise Post-Jogee' by Joanne Cecil & James Mehigan
'A Practical Guide to the Pre-Action RTA Claims Protocol for Personal Injury Lawyers' by Antonia Ford
'A Practical Guide to Neighbour Disputes and the Law' by Alexander Walsh
'A Practical Guide to Forfeiture of Leases' by Mark Shelton
'A Practical Guide to Coercive Control for Legal Practitioners and Victims' by Rachel Horman
'A Practical Guide to the Law of Driverless Cars – Second Edition' by Alex Glassbrook, Emma Northey & Scarlett Milligan
'A Practical Guide to TOLATA Claims' by Greg Williams
'A Practical Guide to Elderly Law – 2nd Edition' by Justin Patten
'A Practical Guide to Responding to Housing Disrepair and Unfitness Claims' by Iain Wightwick

‘A Practical Guide to the Law of Bullying and Harassment in the Workplace’ by Philip Hyland
‘How to Be a Freelance Solicitor: A Practical Guide to the SRA-Regulated Freelance Solicitor Model’ by Paul Bennett
‘A Practical Guide to Prison Injury Claims’ by Malcolm Johnson
‘A Practical Guide to the Small Claims Track – 2nd Edition’ by Dominic Bright
‘A Practical Guide to Advising Clients at the Police Station’ by Colin Stephen McKeown-Beaumont
‘A Practical Guide to Antisocial Behaviour Injunctions’ by Iain Wightwick
‘Practical Mediation: A Guide for Mediators, Advocates, Advisers, Lawyers, and Students in Civil, Commercial, Business, Property, Workplace, and Employment Cases’ by Jonathan Dingle with John Sephton
‘The Mini-Pupillage Workbook’ by David Boyle
‘A Practical Guide to Crofting Law’ by Brian Inkster
‘A Practical Guide to the Law of Domain Names and Cybersquatting’ by Andrew Clemson
‘A Practical Guide to the Law of Gender Pay Gap Reporting’ by Harini Iyengar
‘NHS Whistleblowing and the Law’ by Joseph England
‘Employment Law and the Gig Economy’ by Nigel Mackay & Annie Powell
‘A Practical Guide to Noise Induced Hearing Loss (NIHL) Claims’ by Andrew Mckie, Ian Skeate, Gareth McAloon
‘An Introduction to Beauty Negligence Claims – A Practical Guide for the Personal Injury Practitioner’ by Greg Almond
‘Intercompany Agreements for Transfer Pricing Compliance’ by Paul Sutton
‘Zen and the Art of Mediation’ by Martin Plowman
‘A Practical Guide to the SRA Principles, Individual and Law Firm Codes of Conduct 2019 – What Every Law Firm Needs to Know’ by Paul Bennett
‘A Practical Guide to Adoption for Family Lawyers’ by Graham Pegg
‘A Practical Guide to Industrial Disease Claims’ by Andrew Mckie & Ian Skeate
‘A Practical Guide to Conducting a Sheriff Court Proof’ by Andrew Stevenson
‘A Practical Guide to Vicarious Liability’ by Mariel Irvine
‘A Practical Guide to Applications for Landlord’s Consent and Variation of Leases’ by Mark Shelton
‘A Practical Guide to Relief from Sanctions Post-Mitchell and Denton’ by Peter Causton

'A Practical Guide to Equity Release for Advisors' by Paul Sams
'A Practical Guide to Financial Services Claims' by Chris Hegarty
'The Law of Houses in Multiple Occupation: A Practical Guide to HMO Proceedings' by Julian Hunt
'Occupiers, Highways and Defective Premises Claims: A Practical Guide Post-Jackson – 2nd Edition' by Andrew Mckie
'A Practical Guide to Financial Ombudsman Service Claims' by Adam Temple & Robert Scrivenor
'A Practical Guide to Running Housing Disrepair and Cavity Wall Claims: 2nd Edition' by Andrew Mckie & Ian Skeate
'A Practical Guide to Holiday Sickness Claims – 2nd Edition' by Andrew Mckie & Ian Skeate
'Arguments and Tactics for Personal Injury and Clinical Negligence Claims' by Dorian Williams
'A Practical Guide to Drone Law' by Rufus Ballaster, Andrew Firman, Eleanor Clot
'A Practical Guide to Compliance for Personal Injury Firms Working With Claims Management Companies' by Paul Bennett
'RTA Allegations of Fraud in a Post-Jackson Era: The Handbook – 2nd Edition' by Andrew Mckie
'RTA Personal Injury Claims: A Practical Guide Post-Jackson' by Andrew Mckie
'On Experts: CPR35 for Lawyers and Experts' by David Boyle
'An Introduction to Personal Injury Law' by David Boyle

These books and more are available to order online direct from the publisher at www.lawbriefpublishing.com, where you can also read free sample chapters. For any queries, contact us on 0844 587 2383 or mail@lawbriefpublishing.com.

Our books are also usually in stock at www.amazon.co.uk with free next day delivery for Prime members, and at good legal bookshops such as Wildy & Sons.

We are regularly launching new books in our series of practical day-to-day practitioners' guides. Visit our website and join our free newsletter to be kept informed and to receive special offers, free chapters, etc.

You can also follow us on Twitter at www.twitter.com/lawbriefpub.

www.ingramcontent.com/pod-product-compliance
Lightning Source LLC
LaVergne TN
LVHW022113200926
848481LV00003B/1163